THE SUICIDE SNARE

The Suicide Snare

DEBORAH D. DELBRIDGE

CovenantBridge
Publishing

CovenantBridge Publishing
Author Website: www.DeborahDelbridge.com

Unless otherwise noted, all scripture quotations are from The New King James Version of the Bible. Copyright 1982 by Thomas Nelson, Inc., publishers. Used by permission.

First Printing, 2022

ISBN   979-8-9862183-2-8

Contents

Introduction

In May of 2022, a friend of mine called me because she was desperate for advice. She was about to fly out of the country to visit her sister in France and she wanted help because her sister was suicidal. On that call, several things came to mind that she could do to help her sister. When I hung up the phone, I sensed the Holy Spirit telling me to write a book on depression and suicide.

I am not a licensed psychologist; however, I do incorporate a lot of psychology into my books and articles. Surprisingly, there are several psychological theories that agree with Biblical teachings. However, there are some psychological labels I don't agree with. Demonic oppression causes a lot more wrong behaviors than psychology gives it credit for. Traditionally, psychology doesn't recognize spiritual issues or entities. So, while I do reference some psychology in this book, my main focus is on the spiritual aspects of depression and suicide.

There are good Christian psychologists and psychiatrists out there. I endorse them and encourage you to seek them out if you feel like you should. Several years ago, I asked God if I should get licensed in psychology. God's direction to me at the time was to just obey what He told me to do. Nothing more and nothing else. I could speculate on why He said, "no." But I think the main reason was, He didn't want psychological training to overshadow any spiritual insights that He would direct me to focus on in my writings about human behavior.

As you read this book, ask God to speak to you through it. Some parts of it won't pertain to you but other sections will. Ask God to help you be sensitive to the segments that He may want to highlight to you.

Chapter 1

My Boyfriend's Suicide

When I was in my 20's, I dated a guy for two years that took his own life. He was a wonderful man in so many ways, but he was a tortured soul. He was seeing a psychiatrist who put him on medication, and he was also trying to deal with some repressed memories from his childhood. He was manic-depressive but his psychiatrist didn't have him on bipolar medication. She had him on a regular depressant, Prozac.

My relationship with Fred was an emotional roller coaster. He would be so caring, funny, and charismatic and then he would turn indifferent, withdrawn, and sullen. It seemed like he would be happy for a few weeks and then sad for a week until he snapped out of it and then, he would repeat the cycle.

He had a pattern with his romantic relationships. He would break up, then want to get back together. He had done it with his ex-wife and other girlfriends, and he did it with me.

It got to the point where I wouldn't allow myself to experience the happy times in the relationship because I knew the sad times were coming. Somehow, by not embracing the good moments, it made the bad times more tolerable. He really was a remarkable and noble soul, but the roller coaster was more than most people would tolerate. I couldn't plan any fun activities because his depression would kick in and ruin it. I booked and paid for a weeklong cruise in 1992 but he canceled on me. One year, I planned an amazing New Year's Eve, but he broke up with me earlier in the evening and ruined it. The emotional roller coaster was causing me to feel numb towards him. Sure, I loved him, but I always had to have my emotional wall up so the break-ups wouldn't be too devasting.

I got to the point where I told him that the next time he broke up with me, I was done. I wasn't going to go through another break-up and reconciliation. Well, sure enough, one Saturday morning in January of 1993, he broke up with me. And like clockwork, he tried to reconcile.

I wouldn't do it; I couldn't do it. My emotions were already spent. He tried several times to get back together with me. He would get messages to me through Sharon, our mutual friend. He wanted to talk at the park across from my townhouse. He wanted to meet up for dinner to talk. He would hand Sharon notes for me or tell her to tell me that he was thinking about me.

I met with him when he requested it, but my answer was always same. I didn't want to reconcile. The reason I agreed to meet up with him was I wanted to make sure he was okay emotionally. Our mutual friend, Sharon, had told me that he had tried to commit suicide in the past and I wanted to make sure he wasn't contemplating suicide again. Each time I met with him, he assured me he was okay, and he wouldn't attempt take his own life.

The Angel

My best friend Sharon was also Fred's best friend. Sharon's husband, Darryl, had become a born-again Christian by watching TBN during the time that Fred and I dated. Darryl was a general contractor and one morning as he was going out to his truck to go to work, an angel appeared to him in his garage. The presence of the angel was strong, and Darryl fell against the hood of his truck. The angel told him, "Fred is dead, but he is with the Lord" and then left.

Darryl didn't quite know what to do. Fred had just moved to a different house, and Darryl didn't know where he lived. He took care of an urgent work-related task early that morning and then he called Sharon at work. Sharon didn't mention anything about Fred, so Darryl assumed she didn't know he was dead. Darryl asked her where Fred lived. Sharon thought she knew the area and possibly the street name but didn't have the street number. She wanted to know why he wanted the address but the only thing he told her was that he thought there is something wrong with Fred. Darryl said he needed to find Fred's house, so Sharon insisted on going with him to look for it.

Sharon and I worked at the same company. She called my extension after she hung with Darryl and asked if I had time to take a quick smoke break. We met up at the smoking patio and she told me about her phone call with Darryl. I told her I wanted to go too. She said Darryl didn't want me to go. There was no changing his mind and I had some meetings scheduled, so I told Sharon to call me after they went to his house.

After I finished some back-to-back meetings, I listened to my work voicemails. One of the voicemails was from Darryl telling me to call their house. I called and Sharon answered and said, "Get over here," and hung up.

I knew what had happened without her saying the words. I walked into my boss's office and told him that I had to leave because I thought my ex-boyfriend had just committed suicide. I asked him to tell my team that

I had to leave. The employees that I managed were all on their lunch break and I didn't want to wait until they returned. My boss told me not to worry about anything; he would handle things with my team. He also told me to take the rest of the week off.

Driving over, my legs were trembling. I couldn't control them. The drive over started out in silence, as the whole thing seemed surreal. Then, as I got off the freeway, I started pleading with God for it not to be true.

When I got to Sharon's house, I saw that the garage door was open and the access door from the garage to the kitchen was open as well. I walked in and sat down at the kitchen table. Sharon paced around her kitchen, opening and slamming cabinet doors, and cursing. After a few minutes of venting, she poured us both a vodka tonic and sat down at the kitchen table with me.

She told me what had happened that morning with the angel appearing to Darryl. She told me that they drove over and located Fred's new house. They found the house because Fred's car was in the driveway. They banged on the door, but no one answered. They went through the side yard and started looking through windows. Then, they saw Fred on the floor of his room in a pool of blood. When the police department showed up, they wouldn't let Sharon and Darryl inside the house because they had to treat it as a possible crime scene.

That was one of the worst days of my life. I don't think I have ever cried as hard as I did that day. Friends and neighbors, who knew Fred, all gathered over at

Sharon's house and we all just drank, smoked, and cried. We recounted little clues that we should have picked up on. Some of his friends said that he occasionally talked about suicide, but they thought it was just talk. They didn't believe he would actually plan it out and do it. Other friends who only saw his warm, friendly, and charismatic side were shocked to learn that he struggled with depression because they never saw that side of him.

The Audio Cassette Tape

Fred had left instructions for the coroner's office to release all documentation and his remains to Sharon rather than his biological family. Sharon received a call from the coroner's office telling her about that. They also said that Fred left two manilla envelopes, one for Sharon and one for me. They told her the envelopes would be released when they finished their investigation.

It was during that three-day wait while the coroner completed their investigation, that I realized that Fred died exactly two years to the day that we had started dating. He shot himself through the heart on what would have been our two-year anniversary.

Both Sharon and I received private audiotape cassettes from Fred in our envelopes. My manilla envelope also contained pictures, mementos, and greeting cards I had given to him over the course of our relationship. I was surprised that he kept everything. Every ticket stub from shows we had seen together were there. Birthday cards, valentine cards, and *'just because'* cards were all in there. There was also a handwritten page of lyrics to a Stephen Stills song, called 4+20, that talked about embracing the *Many-colored Beast*. The song was about agreeing with demons! I had too much college psychology to realize it at the time, but when Fred talked about his demons, I assumed it was all metaphorical. I didn't understand that suicidal thoughts originated from actual demons.

The audiotape cassette that Fred left me was very loving and he wanted to make sure I didn't blame myself for his decision to take his life. He said he had been on this course for a very long time. He apologized that being with him was an emotional rollercoaster and he wished it wasn't like that. He also said that he listened to me when I would tell him about God. He said that before he takes his life, he will accept Jesus into his heart. He assured me that he wouldn't take his life until he had made peace with God.

I had grown up in an evangelical church, but I was backslidden during my relationship with Fred. Even though I wasn't living a godly life, I still preached God to Fred.

At his funeral, his sister got up and spoke. She said she read Fred's journal and Fred talked about how he didn't see how he could make a relationship work with anyone, if he couldn't make it work with me. His sister basically blamed me for Fred's death in front of the more than 200 people that were there.

His sister needed a villain, so she blamed me. In fact, during that whole week between his death and the funeral service, people kept trying to play the *blame game*. His family blamed me. His friends blamed his family (because of his terrible childhood). Some of his friends blamed his psychiatrist for prescribing the wrong medication and not keeping a better eye on him. Two of his friends blamed themselves for not picking up on little clues.

The Whys

There wasn't just one issue that convinced Fred to kill himself. I believe there were four factors that played a role.

1) Yes, he wanted to reconcile our relationship and I didn't want to. But we weren't teenagers dealing with our first love. Fred was a 36-year-old divorced man. He had had several girlfriends in his life. It wasn't like our relationship was an all-consuming love story. What bothered him about our break-up was he had bought into the lie that said, "if he couldn't make it work with me, he couldn't make it work with anyone." I have an easy-going personality and I'm not a nag. Yes, I have some good qualities, but I wasn't his perfect woman; and I wasn't his soulmate. If he learned how to break that emotional rollercoaster thing, he could have made someone a wonderful husband.

2) Another huge factor in his suicide was his relationship with his father. He hated him because his father was a drunk. During the time that we were dating, Fred started to see a psychiatrist and he had some repressed memories resurface. Fred remembered that he was forced to live with his father when he was 13 years old after his parents divorced. He remembered some of his father's drunken episodes and he remembered being sexually abused by his father on several occasions.

Fred had a very difficult time processing that discovery. As well, I think the psychiatrist kept pushing him to question his own sexuality. Could the reason he kept breaking up with the women in his life be that he may be gay? I think the psychiatrist was trying to force him to consider that possibility. That wasn't something that Fred wanted to consider. I can say with all confidence that I don't think he experimented sexually as an adult. But it was possible that he could have had unexplored bi-sexual tendencies. At that time, in the early 90's, people with bi or fluid sexuality were told they were lying to themselves. The culture, at that time, refused to accept bisexuality. Bisexuals were told that they were gay, but they just hadn't fully accepted it yet. Today, of course, that viewpoint has changed. Bisexual tendencies and fluid sexuality is accepted. However, the fact that he went along with his father's sexual abuse made him question his sexuality and his whole identity.

I think that is the real reason he broke up with me on that January morning in 1993. I think he was bombarded with new information and new questions, and he needed some time and space to figure it out.

3) Another issue that tormented him was his debt. He had anxiety and He would stew and worry about debt. His debt was under $3,000, yet to him, it may as well have been a million dollars. He would think about and talk about his debt way too much. He had a good, steady job and made decent money. But the whole idea of owing money to a bank terrified him. A little molehill of debt felt like a huge mountain to him. It consumed his peace. Those quiet moments that should have been filled with blissful relaxation, were instead times of re-hearsing how and when he could pay back his debt. He wouldn't let himself have peace; instead, he rehearsed negative, fearful thoughts.

4) The fourth factor in his suicide was his medi-cation. His psychiatrist had Fred on Prozac which is a regular anti-depressant. Fred was clearly bi-polar which was evidenced by his mood cycles, and he should have been on a bi-polar medication. But Fred's psychiatrist thought that since he didn't turn super mean when he was depressed, he wasn't manic-depressive.

Not only was it the wrong medication for his mental issues, but Prozac has a terrible side effect. If a person stops taking it, they could have suicidal thoughts. Fred knew that he wasn't supposed to drink alcohol while on Prozac, so when he started drinking, he stopped taking his medication. His brain chemicals were already out of whack, but discontinuing Prozac cold turkey, sent him into more of a tailspin.

There were four major factors, besides demonic suggestions, that contributed to Fred's decision to take his own life. There could have been more, but there were four that I knew of.

The Funeral

I wasn't scheduled to speak at the memorial service. Why would I be? The family blamed me, and the service was being held at the church Fred's sister occasionally attended. However, Sharon was scheduled to speak, so I got up with her and we went to the podium together. After she gave her eulogy, I shared what was on my heart.

I didn't get up there to point any fingers of blame or deflect any blame away from me. I had asked Sharon if she had planned on sharing what had happened to Darryl with the angel and she said, "no." So, I told her I thought the people should know about it and she agreed with me. I told everyone about the angel appearing to Darryl and I told them what Fred said on his audiotape to me. I shared how he said he wasn't going to do it until he found peace with God. He was going to accept Jesus into his heart. On the audiotape, he recited the sinner's prayer.

About a year after Fred's passing, I ran into a good friend and co-worker of Fred's at a restaurant. He told me that there wasn't a day that went by that he and his co-workers didn't talk about Fred and about what I said at the memorial service.

People that have lost loved ones need to know that just because someone commits suicide, it doesn't mean they automatically go to hell. The Catholic church taught that suicide was the unpardonable sin and that those that took their own life would spend eternity in hell. They taught that wrong doctrine because they wanted to discourage people from committing suicide.

Does God approve of suicide? Of course, not. He has a plan of salvation and a way out of dire circumstances. However, God doesn't reject those that are sick. And God certainly doesn't reject those that have mental sickness. Whether that mental sickness, that despair, is temporary or a longstanding issue, a person's salvation all boils down to their heart condition with God. Have they surrendered their heart to God and invited Him in? Fred verbalized the plan of salvation on the cassette tape. He quoted the prayer he was going to tell God. And by him saying it on the tape, he confessed Christ before others. The Bible says if you confess Jesus before men, you shall be saved. Romans 19:9 says, *"that if you confess with your mouth the Lord Jesus and believe in your heart that God raised Him from the dead, you will* be saved." Matthew 10:32, "Therefore whoever confesses Me before men, him I will also confess before My father in heaven."

Fred's Son

I feel led to mention one other detail. While I dated Fred, I had an abortion in 1992. In 1995, God led me into a season of dealing with abortion in my life. It was a season of repentance but it was also a time of *peeling the onion* so God could bring healing to that area of my heart. I had tucked the abortion thing into a nook and cranny of my heart, and I never emotionally processed the details of it. During that season, God showed me a vision of Fred in heaven with our son. Fred and a little toe-headed toddler were playing kick ball with each other, and they were both laughing. The child looked to be the age he would have been had he been carried full term. Both of their laughs were full of joy and love. It was amazing to watch.

Fred hated the idea of ever becoming a father because of his terrible childhood. He didn't want to bring a child into this world because of the evil, heartache, and pain that so many people experience. I am thankful to God for showing me that vision because it showed me the utter joy that Fred was experiencing by being a father to that little boy in heaven.

Chapter 2

The Psychological Whys

Many of us have had our lives touched by suicide in some way or another over our lifetime. Perhaps we have even contemplated it ourselves. Or maybe a friend or family member has struggled with it. It is not an issue that is isolated to one socio-economic group, race, or age group. Throughout history, there have been people who have taken their own lives and certainly those who thought about it.

According to the CDC, approximately 46,000 people in the U.S. commit suicide every year. Approximately 12.2 million people a year contemplate suicide, 3.2 million people make plans for suicide, and approximately 1.2 million people in the U.S. attempt suicide every year. That information is from 2020 so we don't know how the Covid lockdowns, business shutdowns, and the economic downturn has impacted those numbers, but I would assume the numbers have increased.

Suicide affects all ages. It is the second leading cause of death among people from 10-34 years of age. It's the fourth leading cause of death among people 35-44 years of age. And its fifth leading cause of death among people 45-54 years of age.

Even though most people know someone who struggles with depression and suicide, the average person doesn't have a clue how to help their suicidal friends. The good news is we know more about it now than we used to.

According to the Mayo Clinic's website, depression can be caused from genetics, brain chemicals, or your life situation. Chronic stressful life situations can increase the risk of developing depression if you aren't coping with the stress well.

Although depression can occur once in a life, people typically have multiple episodes. During the episodes, symptoms occur most of the day, nearly every day and may include:

- Feelings of sadness, tearfulness, emptiness, or hopelessness
- Angry outbursts, irritability or frustration, even over small matters
- Loss of interest or pleasure in most or all activities, such as sex, hobbies, or sports
- Sleep disturbances, including insomnia or sleeping too much
- Tiredness and lack of energy, so even small tasks take extra effort
- Reduced appetite and weight loss or increased cravings and weight gain
- Anxiety, agitation, or restlessness
- Slowed thinking, speaking, or body movements
- Feelings of worthlessness or guilt, fixating on past failures or self-blame
- Trouble thinking, concentrating, making decisions, and remembering thing
- Frequent or recurrent thoughts of death, suicidal thoughts, suicide attempts, or suicide
- Unexplained physical problems, such as back pain or headaches

Psychology also has classified depression into seven categories. They are: 1) major depressive disorder (which is clinical depression), 2) a typical depression, 3) persistent depressive disorder, 4) bipolar disorder, 5) postpartum depression, 6) premenstrual dysphoric disorder and 7) seasonal affective disorder. You can look up these types of depression to get more information about them. However, the different categories of depression aren't what I want to focus on.

The Causes

In this chapter, I want to focus on the three things the Mayo Clinic says depression is caused by. They say it is caused by 1) genetics, 2) brain chemicals, or 3) life situations.

· Genetics

When psychology references the cause as genetic, to me that means that someone is hardwired with that propensity towards depression. Their 1) personality temperament may have a bent towards discouragement, 2) they may have a soul iniquity that manifests as discouragement, or 3) they can have a *generational curse* of depression.

Personality Type

The concept of personality temperament types has been around for thousands of years. There are different schools of thought on the subject. But one that has stood the test of time, came from the Greek physician Hippocrates. He developed four basic types into his medical theories (460-370 BCE). From then, and through modern times, they have been modified and used in many theories in medicine, psychology, and literature. The four types are sanguine, choleric, melancholic, and phlegmatic.

We don't even need to go into the 16 Briggs Myers personality temperament types. We can simply look at the four main types that have been around thousands of years.

- The Sanguine type is sociable, talkative, outgoing, and tends to be pleasure seeking.
- The Choleric type is ambitious, logical, goal-oriented, analytical, and tends to have a leadership drive.
- The Melancholic type is self-reliant, thoughtful, extremely reserved, and is often artistic.
- The Phlegmatic type is introverted, calm, unemotional, easygoing, patient, and agreeable.

Of the four personality types, those with the melancholy personality type are much more prone to fall into depression than the other types. A melancholy person is usually more sensitive, introspective, and serious than other personality types. They are rarely satisfied with superficial things. They often spend time analyzing the past and contemplating the future. They are perfectionists and have difficulty settling for anything other than the ideal. They are typically fearful and contemplative. It may take them ten times longer to make decisions. And they often feel misunderstood, misjudged, and wrongly treated.

Surprisingly, according to a recent web search, the melancholy personality type is the largest type out of the four types, with 43.5% of females and 37.5% of males belonging to this group.

That doesn't seem right. That seems way too high. I hope the data was shewed by confusing or leading questions. Certainly, the real number isn't that high. If it is, something has happened to our society or perhaps it's the Mandela Affect. I remember back in the early 90's when I was first taught about personality types, the melancholy type was 20% to 25% of the population. At least, that is how I remember it.

Soul Iniquities

Soul iniquities or *diseases of the soul* is a new concept for some people. I would recommend reading my book *Blind Spots and Wrinkles, (Understanding Our Blind Spots and Behavior Quirks),* to get a much more comprehensive understanding of the topic. However, I will attempt to give a brief overview in this section.

There are 12 *diseases of the soul* that a person may have. They are: 1) pride, 2) fear, 3) unforgiveness and offense, 4) jealousy and envy, 5) rebellion, 6) religious pride, 7) prejudice and hatred, 8) weak willpower, 9) sexual sins, additions, and fetishes, 10) idolatry, 11) greed and selfish ambition, and 12) critical, judgmental, and negative mindsets. They are subconscious propensities toward certain types of sin. Most people have between two to six of them. Some people know they have weaknesses in a specific area, while others could have a blind spot in that area and not be aware that they have it residing in their subconscious mind.

Psychology and the Bible tell us that our motives (our intents) are housed and driven from our subconscious mind. (I will show that in the next chapter) We may rationalize and reason excuses for our thoughts and behaviors in our conscious mind, but our beliefs and behaviors are driven from what we have resident in our subconscious mind. For example, we may have a logical reason for warning our manager about another employee. We may think it is for the good of the company. We may not realize that our true motive could be based out of jealousy. In this scenario, jealousy is a blind spot for the person, and they don't see its influence on their behavior.

When it comes to depression, different soul iniquities can influence its existence. The obvious *disease of the soul* is number 12, the critical, judgmental, and negative mindset. This soul cancer causes the person to meditate on the negative side of things all the time. Their pessimism goes unchecked, and they rehearse everything that seems wrong.

A person with the *disease of the soul* of fear can also sink into depression. Their mind repeats the worst-case scenarios in their mind, and if this mindset isn't changed, it can certainly lead to discouragement and eventually depression.

Pride can be a root cause of discouragement as well. The soul iniquity of pride causes a person to only consider themselves. Their thinking circles around how situations affect them personally. When everything is self, self, self — it is easy to stew on what they are lacking. If they don't stop their negative and selfish thinking, they can easily get discouraged.

A root of jealousy can also lead a person into discouragement. With jealousy, a person also compares themselves to others. They always look over to see that the grass is greener on the other side. Their constant comparison often leads a person to hate what they perceive they are lacking, which can cause them to embrace gloom.

Generational Curses

The concept of *generational curses* may be new to some people. In my own family, my father had a root of unforgiveness and to listen to his stories about his father, it was easy to see my grandfather had it too. And my brother Ken certainly had it. But that particular iniquity didn't show up in all my father's biological children. Generational curses don't necessarily get passed on to all biological children. It probably has a lot to do with how each child processing information and the emotional responses they choose to embrace. I do believe a person can take measures to ensure they don't embrace the same iniquities as their parents by being aware of the issue and monitoring their thoughts and actions.

The concept of generational curses is in the Bible. Exodus 34:6-7 says, *"And the Lord passed before him and proclaimed, 'The Lord, the Lord God, merciful and gracious, longsuffering, and abounding in goodness and truth, keeping mercy for thousands, forgiving iniquity and transgressions and sin, by no means clearing the guilty, visiting the iniquity of the father upon the children and the children's children to the third and fourth generation.'"*

These two verses almost sound contradictory. It talks about God being merciful and forgiving and then it implies our iniquities will be passed on if they aren't cleared. Certainly, a quick little "forgive me" prayer doesn't uproot a stronghold embedded in a person's subconscious mind. Most of us know that uprooting something out of our subconscious mind isn't that easy. Perhaps these verses are suggesting that if a person is aware of their weaknesses and they repent from their soul strongholds, then those strongholds won't turn into *generational curses.* Exodus 34:7 says, *"...by no means clearing the guilty..."* – well, we know that true repentance absolutely clears the guilty. So, awareness of the iniquity and a repentant heart may stop our iniquities from being passed down as generational curses.

If depression is a generation curse in your family tree, there are things you can do to combat it. We do not have to be a victim of how we are hard-wired or what we are genetically predisposed to.

· Brain Chemicals

Fred's suicide had physiological, psychological, and spiritual factors at play. His brain chemicals were out of whack and his mind was under demonic attack. Stopping Prozac helped contribute to his suicidal thoughts. So, in his case, his brain chemicals were definitely off.

However, when it comes to regular depression, brain chemicals can be off as well. According to WebMD: "The brain chemical serotonin is connected to many body functions such as sleep, wakefulness, eating, sexual activity, impulsivity, learning, and memory. Researchers believe that abnormal functioning of brain circuits that involve serotonin as a chemical messenger contribute to mood disorders (depression and bipolar disorder). There are four primary chemicals that can drive positive emotions you feel throughout the day: dopamine, oxytocin, serotonin, and endorphins (sometimes referred to as D.O.S.E.). Brain chemicals affect our emotions, moods, and even clinical diagnosis. Anti-depressants work to correct brain chemicals. There are several different drugs that may all work a little differently, but their function is to change the brain chemicals."

There are some recent studies that contradict the use mood stabilizers that I will reference later in the book. However, the use of medications to treat depression and anxiety has been the primary treatment path for decades.

The "D" Words

Most experts would agree that for most people the road to depression is a progressive one. It starts with the thought life. If a person is meditating on negative thoughts and they don't *course correct* their thought life, they will continue to sink down into deeper levels of despair and hopelessness. Looks at the definitions of these "D" words. They can be viewed as levels of discouragement and depression.

- Dishearten – to cause to lose hope, enthusiasm, or courage
- Disappointment – sadness or displeasure caused by the nonfulfillment of one's hope or expectations
- Discouragement – to lose confidence or enthusiasm
- Despair – the absence of hope
- Depression – feelings of severe despondency and dejection

When someone is discouraged, they can usually get themselves out of a (metaphorical) 3-foot-deep ditch. However, when a person is depressed, it may feel like they are in a 10-foot-deep pit, and that person doesn't think they can get out of it by themselves. When people are in a pit of depression, they often need chemical, psychological, or spiritual help.

Most psychiatrics would say that when someone is in a clinically depressive state, they should be on an anti-depressant. When a person is in that 10-foot-deep pit, their brain chemicals are off, and most professionals would recommend that they take a medication to boost their brain chemistry.

Medications can be helpful, but they are not the *solve-all*. Our brain chemistry follows our thoughts. If we rehearse negative thoughts all day, it changes our brain chemistry and depletes our happy brain chemicals. Brain chemicals are produced by what we think about. What we think about all day can create changes in our brain chemicals. Medications can be helpful, but we have to also change our thought patterns in order to break free of depression or anxiety. If our thinking doesn't change, the medications won't work.

A problem with taking medications is, it can influence our identity. If we wake up in the morning and we rehearse in our mind, "I'm a depressed person," we allow that thought to become part of our identity and therefore make it more difficult to change. A person that struggles with depression or anxiety needs to guard against branding themselves as permanently depressed or anxious in their subconscious mind. They may be going through a season, but that season shouldn't permanently change their self-identity.

· Life Situations

There is no denying that some people go through extremely difficult things that cause them to loss hope and even the will to live. We have seen situations where a husband or wife passes away and their spouse of 40 or 50 years loses their will to live, and they pass away as well.

Others can go through extremely traumatic events where they face a sudden loss of wealth, reputation, or love. They believe their whole world has ended and they embrace the deception that they should end their life.

While others may be riddled with guilt. The mental torment of their failures and weaknesses convinces them that they just want peace. Some people may even believe that they should die for their actions, so they secretly cling to the solution of suicide.

Still others are in a situation where they are in constant pain, and they just want the pain to stop. There doesn't seem to be any relief from their chronic pain, and they are tired of fighting and enduring the life they currently live. They remember back to when they didn't have the constant torment of pain. Their identity refuses to accept the fact that this life of pain is their new normal, and suicide starts to seem like a good alternative.

I have personally never been suicidal, but I totally understand the frustration of wanting pain to stop. The week before and the week after my emergency gall bladder removal surgery in January of 2015, I remember thinking how I was completely fed up with having pain. I didn't have suicidal thoughts, but I remember thinking, at the time, that I understood why some people would consider suicide just to make the constant pain and discomfort stop.

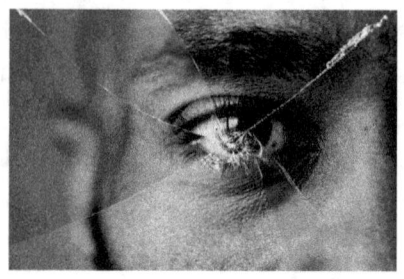

Chapter 3

Understanding Our Soul

As previously mentioned, psychology tells us that our beliefs and behaviors are driven from our subconscious mind, not our conscious mind. With that in mind, it seems like it would be a good idea to study our subconscious mind in a little more detail, so we have a better grasp on what drives our motives, our rationalizations, and our behaviors.

While demonic suggestions play a role in depression and suicide, the greatest influences on our mental health are our own soul deficiencies and our ignorance. All of us are broken in some way or another. All of us have weaknesses and challenges that we contend with. We have emotional wounds, soul iniquities, and self-sabotaging behaviors that weaken, limit, and even deceive us. Most of the time, it's the negative stuff in our soul (conscious mind and subconscious mind) that impairs our success and happiness.

Most Christians would embrace the concept that mankind is a three-part being. We are a spirit. We have a soul. And we live in a body. That definition has been around for decades within the Christian community. Our soul contains our mind, will, emotions, intellect, memory, and creativity. And our human spirit becomes the home where the Holy Spirit resides when we accept Jesus Christ as our savior and make Him the Lord of our lives.

First and foremost, the absence of the Holy Spirit in someone's spirit will cause them to have an inner, intangible loneliness that riches, success, and relationships can't fill. There is an old concept that says, "everyone has a God-shaped hole in their heart." The notion suggests that the human soul has an innate longing for a relationship with God. Some non-believers may challenge this and try to convince you that they are whole and happy. But usually when the party ends, when the lights are out, and when they aren't meditating on the activities of the day, they will acknowledge that they sense something is missing in life.

That longing for a relationship with God goes both ways. God wants to have an interactive relationship with every human on the planet. But unfortunately, the pride that was sired into the human race at the fall of man has deceived mankind. Pride hardens our heart and causes a metaphorical layer of ice between our conscious mind and our subconscious mind. When a person's heart is like a frozen pond, they won't believe the gospel message of salvation. Faith, which is believing something in our heart, our subconscious mind, can't happen unless a person softens their heart towards God. The truth of God's plan can't sink down into their subconscious mind, where true faith resides, if their heart has a hard layer of ice.

Often times, people find a relationship with God when they go through traumatic events in their life. It is in those troubling times that the hard ice of a person's heart is cracked, and that is when they are sensitive to the promptings of the Holy Spirit. When a person feels broken or they are in a situation that they can't fix on their own, that is when they cry out to God for help, and they open their heart to hear from Him.

However, when a person's heart is full of pride, Christianity will seem foolish to them. Their pride will tell them they need all their questions answered first before they would consider embracing the Christian faith. Their arrogance, and maybe even demonic suggestions, will convince them that science and Christianity don't agree. They will go to their grave before acknowledging that some of the greatest scientists that ever lived were

Christians and had a close relationship with God. They will refuse to see what is right in front of them.

As we journey deeper into combatting depression and suicide, it is paramount to acknowledge that having a friendship with God, is more important than anything else. The five things listed below will pertain to you if you are a Christian.

1) You will spend eternity in heaven, not hell.

2) You have the Holy Spirit inside of you, so you won't have a soul emptiness.

3) You will have the ability to learn to hear from God more clearly as you spend time reading the Bible and in prayer.

4) After you receive the baptism of the Spirit, your discernment to hear God's correction, direction, and affection will grow stronger.

5) You can get a revelational understanding of your spiritual authority. Possessing spiritual authority will give you the confidence to command demonic activity out of your life and the lives of those you care about.

Our Subconscious Mind

The phrase *subconscious mind* is a psychological term and isn't used very much in Christian teaching. Christians don't deny that the subconscious mind exists, they just haven't known how to define it since that term is not in the Bible. The Bible uses terms like *heart, mind, soul,* and *spirit* almost interchangeably, and it is up to reader to determine the context of what is being taught. However, when we examine the context of the verse when the word "heart" is used, it usually refers to our inner man which psychology would label as our subconscious mind. So, it may be helpful to think of the term "subconscious mind" when reading your Bible and the word "heart" comes up.

Our subconscious mind is part of our soul and not part of our spirit. Our spirit is the home of the Holy Spirit, and that is the part of us that has been made brand new when we accepted Jesus Christ into our life. We know that our subconscious mind wasn't made completely new when we became a Christian. While some bondages and bad habits may have fallen away, most of us still have bad habits, wrong thoughts, insecurities, and self-sabotaging behaviors.

Our soul has two sections: our conscious mind and our subconscious mind. Our soul still has a carnal nature that we need to *"renew to the word of God"* (in Christian terms, Romans 12:2) or clean up and educate (in worldly terms). We need to renew both our conscious mind and our subconscious mind.

Usually when God talks to us, it isn't with a burning bush or an angelic visitation. Usually, the Holy Spirit speaks to us from our spirit. Guidance from the Holy Spirit will travel from our spirit, through our subconscious mind, and register as a thought in our conscious mind. The problem is most people haven't learned how to recognize the voice of Holy Spirit. Even spiritually mature Christians can have difficulty identifying the voice of the Holy Spirit in their lives. True, some haven't developed their discernment enough to pay attention and hear what God is telling them. But there are a lot of Christians that have flawed discernment because they have too much junk in their subconscious mind. That debris in their subconscious mind can block or distort the subtle promptings of the Holy Spirit that come up from their spirit.

While the Bible doesn't use the term subconscious mind, there is a verse in the Bible that defines it. Hebrews 4:12 reads, *"For the word of God is living and powerful, and sharper than a two-edged sword, piercing even the division between soul and spirit, and of joints and marrow, and is a discerner of the thoughts and intents of the heart."*

Before I talk about the conjunctions in this verse, I want to first comment on the first part of this scripture. It says the word of God is *"living and powerful."* When we read the Bible, new revelations and insights can come to us. The Holy Spirit can highlight a scripture that we have read a hundred times. He can breathe new life on it and cause us to see it in a slightly different way. When Martin Luther read *"the just shall live by faith"* in the Bible in 1517 AD, suddenly, a metaphoric lightbulb turned on. He had a fresh revelation that people are saved by faith and not works. That revelation caused him to confront the Catholic Church and their beliefs, and it was the birth of the Protestant movement. That insight from half of a verse, inspired by the Holy Spirit, changed the direction of Christianity. Even in the last hundred years, the church has gained insights and revelations that earlier Christians didn't have. Millions of people's lives have been impacted by the faith and healing teachings that have been taught and demonstrated. God pours out new revelation all the time, not only to the Church in major ways, but in little ways, giving individual guidance as well.

One day, in the mid-to-late 90's when I was learning about soul iniquities, the Holy Spirit gave me a fresh revelation of this Hebrews 4:12 verse. As I was reading the verse, I sensed the Holy Spirit leading me to take each of the conjunctions and put them into two columns. When I did, a lightbulb flipped on in me. I believe the Holy Spirit illuminated to me that the first column references our conscious mind, and the second column refers to our subconscious mind.

The conjunctions I am referring to are the "and" phrases in the second half of the Hebrews 12:4 verse. They read, *"piercing even the division between (soul and spirit), and of (joints and marrow), and is a discerner of the (thoughts and intents) of the heart."*

Conscious Mind		Subconscious Mind
Soul	and	Spirit
Joints	and	Marrow
Thoughts	and	Intents

Let's look at the first column. The conscious mind is where we think and reason. The Bible's metaphor of a body part describes it as "joint" because the conscious mind is where thoughts are joined together. It is where we reason, where we plan, where we create. The conscious mind is where we connect information, form opinions, organize conclusions, and judge situations. We join together our education with our creativity and think up new ideas, procedures, and strategies. That first column tells us that our conscious mind is where our soul joins our thoughts together.

The second column describes our subconscious mind. To reiterate, psychology tells us that our beliefs and behaviors are driven from our subconscious mind. Our subconscious mind houses our true motives. The word *intent* is another word for motive. So, it appears that the Bible and psychology are in agreement that true motives are originated in the subconscious mind. We may rationalize our biases and opinions in our conscious mind, but our true motives and intents are housed in our subconscious mind.

What is marrow? Marrow is the dark, pasty substance inside of bones. It is hidden and not visible. I think it is so interesting that the Holy Spirit inspired the writer of Hebrews to use these two body parts (joints and marrow) to describe something that he didn't fully understand at the time.

Marrow is that part of the body where red blood cells are produced. The blood that is produced in the marrow is the life force of the entire body. What is made in the hidden part of the body is what carries oxygen and life to every organ, limb, and capillary in the body. Likewise, the substance that is produced in our subconscious mind, is what drives our beliefs and behaviors, and can be witnessed in our words, thoughts, and actions.

The marrow is also where our immunity is strengthened. Our immunity fights sickness and disease, and it is what keeps us healthy. Naturally speaking, when there is disease in the bone marrow, it makes the body weak, sick, and frail. When our immunity is compromised and weak, it shows outwardly, and our poor health is evident for others to see. Likewise, when there is sickness and disease in our subconscious mind, our behavior becomes ugly and evident for others to see.

And lastly, the marrow is where blood platelets are produced. Blood platelets assist in blood clotting, so we don't bleed to death when we are injured. I find this fascinating because our subconscious mind also has types of emotional blood platelets. We have emotional defense mechanisms like denial, repression, compartmentalization, and others that shield us emotionally when we can't handle the full emotional impact of a situation. They stop the emotional bleeding until we can process the psychological trauma in our life.

Conscious Mind (10%)

- Reason and Rationalization
- Create and Strategize

Subconscious Mind (90%)

Psychology tells us our beliefs and behaviors are driven from our subconscious mind. And we may be unaware of our true motives.

Our subconscious mind houses our:

- Our Faith
- Our Rhema Promises and Impartations
- Our Aspirations, Hopes, and Dreams
- Our Personality Temperament
- Our Character Traits
- Our Comfort Zones and Subconscious Limitations
- Our Identity
- Our Fears and Insecurities
- Our Deep-rooted Emotional Wounds
- Our Emotional Defense Mechanisms
- Our Diseases of the Soul/Soul Iniquities (Spots)
- Our Autopilot, Repeating, Neurological Glitches (Wrinkles)

Human Spirit -
Home of the Holy Spirit

The Human Psyche

Our subconscious mind houses both positive and negative substances. It is the home and incubator for our: 1) Faith, 2) Rhema Promises and Impartations, 3) Aspirations, Hopes, and Dreams, 4) Personality Temperament, 5) Character Traits, 6) Comfort Zones and Subconscious Limitations, 7) Identity, 8) Fears and Insecurities, 9) Deep-rooted Emotional Wounds, 10) Emotional Defense Mechanisms, 11) *Diseases of the Soul* or Soul Iniquities (Spots), and 12) Our Autopilot, Repeating, Neurological Glitches (Wrinkles).

Our Computer

If we look at the attached graphic, we will see that (according to psychology) 10% of our soul is our conscious mind and the other 90% is our subconscious mind. We don't know the actual percentages, but it isn't relevant. The point is, we have a part of our mind that is hidden from our awareness. I think we can understand the human psyche better if we look at the components of a computer.

Our spirit, the core of our being, where the Holy Spirit resides, is like the motherboard. Our subconscious mind is like the hard drive that stores all information and contains all our programming. Our conscious mind is like the monitor where we are able to see some of what has been loaded on the computer. We can see stored pictures and documents; allowing us to access and use programs that are on the hard drive. A monitor only displays some of what has been stored and programmed on a hard drive. Likewise, our conscious mind only allows us to see some of what has been stored and programmed in our subconscious mind.

We can access information online and view it on our monitor. We can see pictures, stories, theories, and ideas that we understand and agree with but just because we can agree with it on our monitor, doesn't mean that content has been downloaded and saved to our hard drive. Most people think that what they believe and agree with in their conscious mind is downloaded onto their subconscious mind and that isn't the case. We may believe something in our head but that doesn't mean we believe it in our heart (our subconscious mind). We make the mistake of thinking that the sermons we hear and agree with are downloaded onto our hard drive, our subconscious mind, and they aren't. Just like the programs and information we access online are viewed on our monitor, but they are not downloaded on our hard drive.

And finally, the keyboard represents programming. Words, symbols, numbers, and functions keys are used to write programming codes that modify what is on the computer. Not everything that is typed changes a computer's programming. Just like not everything that is said, read, or heard changes our subconscious mind. However, programming is changed by words. Hebrews 10:17 says, *"Faith comes by hearing and hearing by the word of God."* What is faith? Faith is believing something in our subconscious mind, our gut, whether that belief is something good or it is something negative. Hearing the word of God can actually program faith into our subconscious mind. As well, hearing negative words can program our subconscious mind in a harmful way.

Viruses and Glitches

Just like we can have a virus on a hard drive that affects the performance of a computer, we can have viruses and glitches in our subconscious mind. *Diseases of the soul* are like computer viruses. *Diseases of the soul* are soul iniquities that were discussed briefly in the second chapter. They are diseased spots in our subconscious mind that can get triggered in certain situations. They are subconscious strongholds, that we may not be aware of, that are dictating and driving some of our thoughts and behaviors.

To refresh your memory, the soul iniquities are: 1) pride, 2) fear, 3) unforgiveness and a spirit of offense, 4) jealousy and envy, 5) rebellion, 6) religious pride, 7) prejudice and hatred, 8) weak willpower, 9) sexual sins, additions, and fetishes, 10) idolatry, 11) greed and selfish ambition, and 12) critical, judgmental, and negative mindsets.

Everyone has the soul iniquity of pride. It was sired into the bloodline at the fall of man. However, not everyone has the other eleven of them. Some soul iniquities are more common than others. Most people have between two and six of these strongholds in their subconscious mind. They are soul cancers that when left of treated can cause death to relationships, careers, and God-ordained assignments. Like cancer, there can be different kinds and exist at different stages.

The definition of a glitch just means a mistake or irregularity. Do you remember in the first Matrix movie when Neo saw a black cat walk by the doorway, then he saw that exact same thing happen again? He was told that was a *glitch in the matrix* and to beware when that happens. In the movie, when someone experiences a *déjà vu* happening, it was a glitch in the Matrix.

In my book, *Blind Spots and Wrinkles*, a glitch is a repeating belief or behavior that is prompted by bad programming in our subconscious mind. For those of us that are old enough to remember vinyl records, when there is a scratch on the record, it causes the same line to repeat over and over. And believe or not, most of us have autopilot type behaviors that we repeat even though those behaviors are either sinful or self-sabotaging. These glitches (scratches, lines, folds, wrinkles) in our subconscious mind can get triggered when we encounter a situation, emotion, or feeling that we have had in the past. As a result, we just repeat the belief or behavior in almost an autopilot manner. And negative beliefs and behaviors that repeat in an almost autopilot manner are like glitches on a computer's hard drive.

Neuroscience

Neuroscience tells us that streams of beliefs and patterns of behavior are established pathways in our mind. There are so many pathways that it only makes sense that we have ones that are not beneficial for us. But thank God, neuroscience also tells us we can *train our brain* and replace negative pathways with new positive ones. The biggest problem is most of our negative beliefs or behaviors go unchecked and unchallenged. They are rarely diagnosed. And they are usually not understood, so they are not dealt with properly.

A neuroscience instructor who was conducting a training that I attended, called our patterns of behavior *pathways in the brain,* but in my mind, I envisioned them like a complex freeway system. The last time I was in Dallas, I was completely amazed by the complexity of all of the highways, byways, overpasses, and offramps in the downtown Dallas area. It was a mess. Even with my navigational app on my phone, I still took wrong exits and ended up on streets I didn't want to be on. I immediately drew a parallel between the Dallas freeway system and the neuroscientist's pathways in the brain analogy. If we think of our patterns of thoughts and behaviors like a giant roadway complex, we can understand how we can keep taking the wrong offramps of negative conclusions and behaviors.

In certain situations, we don't pay attention. Our mind is on other things as we take the roads (pathways) we are familiar with. We have all driven with our minds on other things and we have missed the offramp we had intended to take. Or, we have driven home on autopilot and forgot that we had intended to run an errand before going home. We weren't thinking about our driving as we were driving. Our mind was on something else. Yet, our internal autopilot kicked in as we thought about something that happened at work or a conversation we had with a friend. After I moved to my current house, there were a couple of times where I had accidentally driven into my old tract. The same is true for our thought patterns and negative behaviors. We take the offramps we are used to, even if it means we end up at destinations that weren't intended. They are our *normal*. And we are often blind to the fact that we need to establish a new *normal*.

Our Soul and Depression

In its most basic definition, depression happens when hopelessness is embraced. The absence of hope makes the heart sick. Proverbs 13:12 says, *"Hope deferred makes the heart sick, but when the desire comes, it is a tree of life."* The disappointments of life can steal the hope that is in our heart. That is why we need to take heed to ourselves and guard our hearts. We cannot let the enemy of our soul, or our life circumstances take our hope, fortitude, and strength.

Proverbs 4:20-22 says, *"My son, pay attention to my words; incline your ear to my sayings. Do not let them depart from your eyes; keep them in the midst of your heart; for they are life to those who find them, and health to all their flesh. Keep your heart with all diligence, for out of it springs the issues of life."*

We need to keep our heart with all diligence. Our soul is strengthened when we pay attention to the word of God and incline our ear to it. Inclining our ear means we listen for the Holy Spirit to speak to us through the Word. It keeps our hope and faith strong. The word of God breathes life into our soul. It brings physical health and emotional health. We can take heed to ourselves and keep our heart with all diligence, so we don't embrace defeat and hopelessness.

Philippians 4:6-7 says, *"Be anxious for nothing, but in everything by prayer and supplication, with thanksgiving, let your requests be made known to God; and the peace of God, which passes understanding, will guard your heart and minds through Christ Jesus."* When we are in constant fellowship with God, He will pour peace into our heart. A peace that the world can't understand will guard our heart. That peace will protect our heart from distress, anxiety, and fear. Negative circumstance can hit us, but the peace of God will insolate us from fear and worry and it will mystify those around us. Others won't understand why we are not freaking out with fear.

As we read earlier, faith comes by hearing the word of God. Reading the Bible and fellowshipping with the Holy

Spirit, literally deposits faith and hope into our subconscious mind. Remember, our goal in renewing our mind is to make good deposits of substances into our subconscious mind, while we uproot the negative junk. Wow, that almost makes it sound like spending time with God can cure depression. Yep! It can.

Taking heed to ourselves can help as well. If we know we have a stronghold of jealousy and we know that our mind wants to constantly compare ourselves to others, then we won't be as quick to beat ourselves up when we don't measure up in a specific area. Or if we know we have a *disease of the soul* of unforgiveness, we will think twice before we allow someone's comment to hurt our feelings. We can see the issue from a different angle and choose not to let it hurt us as much. If we know we have a melancholy personality, we can take active measures to stop the negative self-talk. Knowing ourselves, understanding how our minds work, and having quality time with God, will dramatically reduce the occurrences of depression.

Chapter 4

The Nudge Factors

In the last chapter, it was mentioned that our personality type or our soul iniquities can significantly impact our propensity for depression. However, in this chapter, we are going to go a little deeper and discuss other challenges, situations, and life events that may nudge us towards discouragement or depression.

Normally, a person doesn't wake up one day and suddenly feel suicidal. There is usually an extended period of time where a person experiences a soul sadness.

And that depression can be magnified by a persistent situation they are dealing with that inches them closer towards the desire to give up. That nudge factor can be known by the person's family and friends, or it may be a private struggle.

Anxiety

Anxiety is the mind and body's reaction to stressful, dangerous, or unfamiliar situations. It's a sense of uneasiness, distress, or dread a person can feel before a significant event. Experiencing occasional anxiety is a normal part of life. However, people with anxiety disorder frequently have excessive fear and worry.

It is estimated that 40 million Americans have anxiety disorder, so roughly 12% of the population in the United States have it. Some people believe there is a connection between anxiety and suicide. One study showed that 70% of the people that attempted suicide were also diagnosed with anxiety.

Those of us that don't have anxiety disorder may have a difficult time understanding why people are trapped by it. I know and have known people with anxiety disorder and for them, their mind just starts to panic even in non-stressful situations. With one young woman I know, her heart will start beating fast and her emotions will tell her brain to panic and fear even when there is nothing unusual happening. I have talked to her while she was having anxiety episodes to try to understand what she was feeling and thinking. And surprisingly, even normal activities that she is comfortable with, can suddenly cause her to panic.

Another male friend of mine has anxiety as well. For him, when he is feeling anxious, he feels very antsy, and he has a compulsion to leave where he is. The need to leave is a common occurrence with him. He has felt it while he was at his home, not just places that were unfamiliar or uncomfortable for him.

I recognize that anxiety disorder is a psychological condition, however, I suspect that those that have it also have the *disease of the soul* of fear. Certainly, the people I know now and have known in the past that have anxiety disorder, also have a stronghold of fear in their subconscious mind.

If we look at the symptoms, it appears that anxiety is the body's physical reaction to fear. Common anxiety disorder symptoms are:

1) feeling nervous, restless, or tense,
2) having a sense of impending danger, panic, or doom,
3) having an increased heart rate,
4) breathing rapidly (hyperventilation),
5) sweating,
6) trembling,
7) feeling tired or weak,
8) trouble concentrating,
9) trouble sleeping,

10) having gastrointestinal problems,

11) having difficulty controlling worry,

12) Having an urge to avoid things that trigger anxiety.

Depending on what an anxious person is worrying about, it may nudge them towards considering suicide. Fred, my boyfriend that killed himself, had anxiety. There were a couple of times where he actually had panic attacks, which had symptoms similar to a heart attack. My brother Ken had panic attacks a few times as well. When someone's mind just keeps circling the same concerning thoughts over and over again, they can get caught up in a false reality and their physical body reacts.

Lonely

Loneliness can be another nudge factor. I went through a lonely season in my life in my mid-20s and I would even say that it was a season of depression. Even though I was raised in church, I backslid when I was 19 years old. There was a ten-year period where I wasn't close to God, as I mentioned earlier in this book. I dated a guy for five and a half years (from 19 years old to 25 years old) but when he broke up with me, I went into a season of isolation. The relationship needed to end. It was at a dead-end. I never considered marrying him. But we stayed together because we were comfortable with each other. The problem was, I spent all my time with him, and my other friendships had fallen away. So, after the breakup, I was alone and lonely.

I was working at the computer manufacturer at the time, but my life was in a rut. I went to work, came home, read a few chapters of a book, or watched TV, went to bed, and did it all again the next day. I just felt numb. I read books and watched TV to escape and fill the time. I didn't have anyone in my life that I felt close to or that I talked to on a regular basis. While I have been very close to my sisters at different seasons, I wasn't close to them at that time. Occasionally, I would cry, but I mostly just felt numb as I turned off all emotion. After the breakup, I started going out to breakfast on Saturday mornings with my sister Barbara, but we weren't that close. We didn't share very many details of our lives with each other.

My lonely, depression season lasted about a year and a half. It finally broke when I started hanging out with Sharon. At work, I was transferred to a different team and Sharon was on that team. She was outgoing, friendly, and very charismatic and we soon became good friends. Surprisingly, my personality blossomed around Sharon. I became friendly, outgoing, and charismatic. (And Sharon, of course, was the friend that introduced me to her friend Fred.)

Humans are social beings. We need each other and it isn't emotionally healthy for a person to be isolated. Loneliness can happen when there is an absence of close interaction with other people.

Since then, there have been a few seasons of my life where I have been alone. There have been times when I have had a best friend and other close friendships, and other seasons where I didn't really feel close to anyone.

I fully surrendered my life to God in June of 1994. In May of 1995, I was shunned by Bible college students that I had become friends with. I was in an alone season again. But it was different than it was when I wasn't close to God. I was alone but didn't feel lonely. I had received the Baptism of the Holy Spirit, and I had developed a friendship with God. God knew the rejection I was facing, and He spoke to my heart and loved on me.

That was a tumultuous season for me. My circumstances were such that I had to walk by faith. I had to stay close to God, so I knew what steps to take and what steps to avoid. My life was in a storm, and I had to stay in the eye of the storm where it was calm, in order to survive. I had to development my discernment to hear from God because it felt like I was marching through a minefield.

I remember in June of 1995, I sensed that God wanted me to finally take Fred's ashes to Carmel in Northern California. I had his ashes with me for two years waiting for the right time to take them to the location that he told me he wanted his ashes spread. So, I went on a road trip by myself from Southern California to Northern California. The trip felt very surreal. It was like I took a road trip with God. As I saw different sites, I would talk to God about them. The motel I had reserved was seedy and in a bad part of town (because I was on a budget). Even though I could hear sirens and people yelling, I didn't have any fear because it felt like it was part of my adventure with God.

I am sharing this story with you to make a point. Sometimes, it takes a lonely season, to discover the presence of God in our lives. When we have too many friends and family around us, it is easy for us to rely on them for their love, support, and guidance. But God wants to be closer than a brother to us. He wants to have that number one position in our hearts. And that closeness is developed in hard times. Even though that season could be considered a "dark night of the soul," it was a season I now cherish. I still remember seeing a beautiful waterfall on that road trip and crying because I didn't have anyone to share the moment with. God spoke to me and said He was sharing it with me. Truly, does it get any better than that? People often bring disappointments but when God is your best friend, He never disappoints. In the alone times of your life, lean into God. Purposely and intentionally, develop your discernment to hear His voice. Spend time in the Bible, let the Holy Spirit whisper encouragement to your heart through the word.

Seasons come and go. People in your life come and go. But God remains and He can fill any and every void in your life.

Loss of a Loved One

Another nudge factor that a person can have in their life is the tremendous sense of loss that comes when they lose a loved one. We have all heard stories of couples that have been married for many years and one of them passes, and the other one passes shortly after. When a person has spent decades married to the same person, their absence is immense. The grieving spouse doesn't know how to live without them. Their souls were so connected, living without them seems too hard. Many grieving spouses lose the will to live.

A parent losing a child can have the same effect. Some parents sink into a deep depression at the loss of a child, and some even lose the will to live.

Some people experience that devastating loss when they lose a pet. I know my brother Ken was devastated for months when he lost his dog, Colonel Puppy Ruff, who literally was best friend. He was even a little suicidal after his dog passed away.

Experiencing loss can affect people in different ways. For some people, the loss is felt on a deeper level and can shatter their mental well-being.

Betrayal

Many of us have experienced betrayal in one form or another. Maybe we have had a husband, wife, boyfriend, or girlfriend that cheated on us. Maybe a co-worker sabotaged us or took credit for our work. Perhaps a business partner embezzled money.

There is no getting around it. We will have disappointments in life. We know what it is to trust and care for someone, only to discover that they have betrayed us. It is in those times, that the demon assigned to us will try plant negative thoughts and make the emotional wound greater than it needs to be.

When we go through a betrayal, we need to keep our emotions in check. If we allow a root of unforgiveness to set it, it can limit our healing and interfere with our relationship with God. Unforgiveness is a big deal to God. Matthew 6:15 says, *"But if you do not forgive men their trespasses, neither will your Father forgive your trespasses."* Unforgiveness can easily link arms with pride and make us think we have a right to be offended. If we aren't careful, we can adopt deceptive thinking and add details that aren't true and even whitewash our role in the situation in our imagination. We start to believe that what that person did was so terrible, they don't deserve forgiveness. We somehow forget our own shortcomings and just focus on how we have been wronged. That heart posture hardens our heart and can impair our relationship with God. When our heart is hard, we can't hear the Holy Spirit, so we start to backslide in our heart.

Once out of fellowship with God, we can open to door to deceptive thinking and embrace depression. Betrayal isn't always a nudge factor towards depression, but it can certainly be the vehicle that gets us to that frame of mind.

Disappointment in Self

Most of us have things about ourselves that we would like to change, whether it's our appearance, health, behavior, or anything else about ourselves. We don't point the finger of blame at others, but rather we are disappointed in ourselves.

When it comes to trying to change a behavior, we may have tried a hundred times, but old patterns kick in and we just return to the same self-sabotaging actions. Maybe we made plans to diet but there were donuts at work and the diet plans flew out the window. Possibly alcohol has its grip on us, and good intentions are procrastinated as we pour ourselves another glass of wine. We can decide something but then find ourselves doing the opposite thing an hour later. There is a disconnect between our will and our behavior.

The Apostle Paul wrote about this in Romans 7:15. The verse reads, *"For what I am doing I do not understand. For what I will to do, that I do not practice; but what I hate, that I do."* The last chapter talked about our beliefs and behaviors being driven from our subconscious mind, not our conscious mind. So, our good intentions are doomed to fail unless we work on our subconscious mind.

Being disappointed in ourselves doesn't just happen because we have bad habits. Often, people carry deep-rooted regrets because their actions could have hurt someone, or they may regret a decision they made. Some people have a difficult time moving past their wrong decisions and they live in the torment of regret. That weight of regret can get heavy and soon they have a heaviness of heart and a soul sadness.

People that are perfectionists have a harder time with this. They are idealist and they are hard-wired to expect excellence from others and themselves. For those people, disappointments carry a greater burden than they do with other personality temperament types. When they don't see their reality lining up with what they have envisioned for themselves, they can get very despondent.

A friend of mine in the 2000's was very idealistic. She was a wonderful Christian gal who even rented a room from me for a bit while she attended Bible School. She was on fire for God. She preached in convalescent homes and went out witnessing. She was very passionate in everything she did. However, in 2009, when many Christians were experiencing a spiritually dry season, she isolated herself and went into depression. She wasn't happy with her life because it wasn't what she had thought it should or could be. She ended up hanging herself. She didn't want to live in a world where she wasn't living the life she had thought she would have.

While she is in heaven and her family and friends will see her again, Chrissy didn't have to end her life. She was going through a season, and seasons change. She could have become what she envisioned herself to be. But she let a temporary setback take her out.

Sense of Identity

I talk a lot about our identity in my book, *Blind Spots and Wrinkles*, and I focus on the impact of identity-shaping words and how they can change who we are. However, in this section, I want to address how our identity, or our lack of it, can affect our soul.

There used to be a saying in the 70's that said, "I need to go find myself." It usually entailed getting away from your current situation on a quest to discover yourself and identify your passion, skill, vocation, or purpose in life.

Having a sense of identity is important. Without it, most people will question their value and purpose for living. Some people compare themselves to others to evaluate and validate themselves. They may hold other people up as benchmarks and think they can only achieve what they see others achieving.

A person that doesn't understand their value and their purpose may act confident but deep down, they aren't. They don't understand their value to God. In their conscious mind, they believe God loves them but in their subconscious mind, they don't have that certainty. Many of them base their value on performance or appearance. Because they don't have a strong sense of identity, the opinions of other can easily affect them. A criticism can send their self-esteem into a downward spiral.

We must remember that each of us are *"fearfully and wonderfully made,"* (as it says in Psalms 139:14). God didn't mess up when He made us. All of us have attributes and flaws.

A person that doesn't know who they are is more sus-ceptible to depression. I don't think it is a coincidence that the trans community has a high rate of attempted suicide. Studies show that transgender people are two times more likely to attempt suicide than lesbian, gay, or bisexual people. The concept of gender fluidity may seem like a good idea to some people, but it removes the foundation of a person's identity. Think about it. Why do you think those DNA ancestry kits are so popular? There is an innate desire to know who we are. We want to know the percentages of the different nationalities that are in us. We want to know if we are related to any historically famous people. It's hard to build the walls of our identity if our concrete foundation has cracks in it. A person that is gender fluid, where they feel male one day and then female the next, doesn't have a foundation of identity. Without a firm foundation of the raw basics, they will have a difficult time framing the rest of their identity.

Knowing who we are is important. But it is also important to know our purpose. Why are we here on Earth? Why were we born? What are our assignments to help humanity? This all goes back to that God-shaped hole in our hearts.

When a person knows what it is to hear God's voice for themselves, and to know some of the assignments He has for them, that understanding helps them make sense of their whole existence. There is an inner satisfaction and contentment when we know who we are and why we are here.

Overwhelmed by Concerns

Some people allow the cares of this world to steal their peace and convince them that their problems are more than they can bear. People have committed suicide over an argument they had with their boss, over not being able to pay a bill, and over fear of a legal issue. They allow their negative emotions to not only rule them, but to lie to them.

If a person stews, meditates, and worries over situations and circumstances, they empower the kingdom of darkness to rule in their life. What you think about is your choice. If you choose to rehearse your concerns over and over again in your mind, you make that problem much bigger than it needs to be.

Almost every problem or situation in our life is like a diamond. It is multifaceted. It has several sides, details, and perspectives. When we rehearse our viewpoint of the situation, we typically just focus on one side. We focus on the details that support our offense and we overlook other details about the situation. We make one facet or side way bigger than all the other details of the situation so our perspective can get distorted. The issue we are focusing on may be true, but when we aren't considering other details about the situation, we are not seeing the issue clearly. We can turn a minor incident into a major life crisis by what we choose to believe about it. And when people believe their version of reality is the whole truth, they are more susceptible to delusional thinking, and they can sink into a pit of despair.

Pain

Another nudge factor can be pain, illness, or injury. A person that lives day in and day out in constant pain, has a challenge that many of us can't relate to. I know people that have painful diseases that they struggle with all day, every day. For them, the mental struggle is as difficult as their physical battle. Some people in that situation, lose the will to live.

That was the case with my brother, Ken. He was in the hospital because of liver and kidney failure. He had started to make some improvements but then the hospital was negligent in their care for him. He went four or five days without food or water when he was in the I.C.U.. They didn't want to give him water because his body wasn't producing urine. When I visited him, he would beg me for water, but the hospital wouldn't give it to him.

They didn't give him food for five days because they wanted to schedule a colonoscopy. They literally gave Ken that overnight laxative three days in a row to prepare for the procedure even though he hadn't had anything to eat or drink. They kept giving it to him because that was their procedure. He had clear diarrhea for days with stomach cramping while the ICU nurses allegedly tried to schedule a GI doctor that would do a simple colonoscopy. Because this took place over a long four-day 4th of July weekend, my brother Ken just had to wait with no food or water until somebody did their job. If they were that negligent with me calling the hospital administrators and advocates, it makes me wonder what kind of care the patients got that didn't have family fighting for them.

As well, Ken's liver condition caused a terrible rash to flare up that was extremely painful, but they wouldn't give him any pain medication. Ken was in agony, and he often screamed in pain, but they wouldn't give him pain medication because they thought it would impact his liver somehow. Ken cried in agony, but the hospital staff acted like they didn't care. There was no empathy and it appeared like they viewed Ken as an annoyance. After two days of requesting it, I finally got them to apply a topical pain ointment to the rash. Why was I the one that came up with that idea? Why did it take them two days to get the doctor's approval for it? They didn't think of a topical pain reliever because they were busy, and they didn't care.

Because Ken's kidneys weren't working correctly, he needed to have dialysis two or three times a week. I'm sure you are supposed to take a patient's blood pressure before administering dialysis. However, I am not sure if they did. If they did, they didn't pay attention to the fact that it was too low to administer dialysis on Ken. They should have given him a pint of blood before they started dialysis because without enough blood in his body, his heart would crash. Well, that is what happened. Ken's heart crashed during dialysis because he didn't have enough blood in his body. They brought him back and had him in an induced coma on a ventilator. However, he passed later that day.

Was it the hospital's fault that Ken died when he did? Yes. Their mistake of not giving him blood before dialysis killed him. However, as I was driving out to the hospital to visit him the day his heart crashed, the Holy Spirit gave me a word of knowledge that Ken had asked God to let him die. He couldn't handle the pain, and really the torture, that the hospital was putting him through. So, in light of Ken's request to pass, I can't get too angry at the hospital for negligently failing to give him blood before the dialysis. They were completely negligent, but it was the mercy of God that allowed Ken to pass when he requested it. Ken didn't want to fight anymore.

I feel led to share this detail as well. When I got to the hospital room and Ken was in an induced coma, I started talking to him. When I asked him questions, he had quite a bit of lip movement. It absolutely appeared like he was trying to respond back to me. Had his lips been moving the whole time, I don't know that I would have had as much certainty. But his lips moved after I asked him questions.

So, if you have a loved one that is in an induced coma, do not assume they can't hear you. I have prayed the "sinner's prayer" with two other people that were in induced comas, and I thought that God allowed them to hear me at the time. But seeing Ken's response, gave me more confidence that people in comas do hear you.

Death for a Christian isn't a terrible thing. They get to step into a pain-free existence where peace and joy abound. And when a person is in terrible pain, the idea of passing can look more appealing than their desire to stay alive.

However, it is not our place to decide when it's our time to pass. That decision belongs to God. My other brother had a word of knowledge that Ken could recover, and his condition didn't have to be fatal. I believe that was a word from God. A good friend of mine has a boyfriend that had the exact same condition as Ken, and he had a complete recovery without a liver transplant. But Ken lost the will to live because of pain, and in God's mercy, He granted Ken's request.

Demonic Oppression

The final nudge factor I want to address is demonic oppression. The spirit world is around us all the time. That old illustration of an angel sitting on one shoulder and a devil sitting on the other, trying to influence our behavior, is more true than people realize.

Most people would agree that we have at least one guardian angel. Well, if God has assigned an angel to us, it is difficult to imagine that the kingdom of darkness would assign a demon to us, as well?

When someone is buffeted with discouraging thoughts on a consistent basis, they may not have a demon in them, but certainly there can be a demon near them tormenting their mind. I do not know the percentage of Christians that have a demon in them verses there being an external demon that makes demonic suggestions. When we have negative thoughts about ourselves or others and we think it is just our own self-talk, it can be demonic suggestions masquerading as our own thoughts.

The concept of a Christian having a demon in them is a controversial one. Some Christian denominations like Presbyterian, Baptist, Methodist, Lutherans, and some Evangelical churches, do not believe Christians can have demons residing in them. They also tend to embrace the stance that some of the teachings and practices of

Jesus and the first century Christians no longer apply to the church today like: the laying on of hands for healing, speaking in tongues, prophesying, and deliverance (casting out demons). Whereas most Spirit-filled denominations like the Assemblies of God, Four Square, Church of God, Calvary Chapel, Vineyard, and Pentecostal churches, do acknowledge the activities of demons and the practices of the first century church. But the degree of their belief and the amount they are practiced can vary quite a bit between the denominations and even individual churches. Most Spirit-filled churches believe the instructions Jesus gave His disciples also apply to us. Jesus said in Mark 16:17-18, *"These signs will follow those who believe: In My name they will cast out demons; they will speak with new tongues; they will take up serpents; and if they drink anything deadly, it will by no means hurt them; they will lay hands on the sick, and they will recover."* (While there are some people who literally handle snakes, most spirit-filled believers do not condone the practice. The dean of the second Bible school I attended went into a lengthy dissertation on why the literal translation of "will take up serpents" should really be translated "will drive away serpents.") Anyway, it was Jesus' instruction to His followers to cast out demons, pray in tongues, and pray healing over those who are sick.

I grew up in an evangelical church that dismissed healing, tongues, and deliverance. We were taught that spirit-filled, charismatic Christians were emotional, weird, and scripturally unbalanced. Demons weren't discussed except to say that a Christian can't have one. I was shocked when I came back to God, after being back-slidden for almost ten years, to learn how much the New Testament talked about tongues, healing, and demons.

Even though I grew up in a church that didn't believe a Christian can have a demon residing in their soul, there was never a question about it in my life. Throughout my life, everyone in my family was a Christian, yet I witnessed demons manifesting through my father and my brother on several occasions. They both had anger demons. When they would get mad and they allowed that rage to manifest, their eyes would glaze over, and their demons would express themselves.

Both Bible schools I attended taught that a Christian can be oppressed by a demon but not be possessed by one. A Christian can have a demon in their soul and but not in their spirit where the Holy Spirit resides. The Bible colleges taught that possession is where a demon has taken residence in a person's spirit and that demon can manifest anytime it wants without the permission of the host human. Oppression is where a demon either hovers around the person externally or it has attached itself to the person's soul with their agreement. When a person is oppressed by a demon, they still have control of their own actions. They have the authority to choose to allow that demon to manifest through them or to shut it down.

More than 25 years ago, I heard a teaching at the second Bible school that I attended that has always stuck with me. The dean of that Bible school, Larry Matteson, taught that we need to be aware of the random thoughts that cross our minds because demons can try to plant wrong thoughts. He used the analogy of a screen door. We open the window or door to get fresh air, but we should always (metaphorically) keep the screen doors closed. The *screen door* thing was part of his teaching out of 2 Corinthians 10:5, that tells us that we need to *take every thought captive*. The verse reads: *"casting down arguments and every high thing that exalts itself against the knowledge of God, bringing every thought into captivity to the obedience of Christ."*

What does that mean? It means we must pay attention to the thoughts that cross our minds. We shouldn't welcome every random thought that wanders across our brain. We should have the *screen door* shut so we don't let the bugs in.

One of the names of Satan is *Beelzebub*, which is translated as *Lord of the Flies*. Demons can operate like a bunch of annoying flies. They fly around our head and try to land on us, meaning try to plant thoughts of negativity, strife, and failure. Ignorant people think that all the thoughts that cross their minds are their own thoughts. They don't know demonic suggestions try to masquerade as our thoughts. Afterall, it is the demons' job to steal, kill, and destroy from us as the Bible says in John 10:10. Their job becomes so much easier if they get us to self-sabotage, so we don't know our negative thoughts are their handiwork.

The spirit world operates by agreement. Angels are activated when we agree with the word of God and speak it out. Psalms 103:20 says, *"Bless the Lord, you His angels, who excel in strength, who do His word, heading the voice of His word."* Angels harken to the word of the Lord. That means that when we speak Bible verses over our situation, we empower angels to work on our behalf. When we agree with the word of God, that agreement activates angels to fight off the darkness that would try to steal, kill, and destroy.

Likewise, demons are allowed access when we agree with demonic suggestions. When someone is discouraged and all they do is meditate on and agree with negative thoughts, that can invite a depression demon into their life. Does everyone that is depressed have a demon in their soul? No, however, that dark cloud hanging over a person's head may not just be a metaphorical one.

Ephesians 6:12 says, *"For we do not wrestle against flesh and blood, but against principalities, against powers, against rulers of the darkness of this age, against spiritual host of wickedness in heavenly places."* Even if we are not hearing demonic suggestions masquerading as our own self-talk, we need to be alert and aware to the fact that we have an enemy that hates us. The flat tire, the misunderstanding at work, the IRS audit, an all the other dramatic situations in our lives, may not all just be coincidences. They can all be the wiles of the devil trying to overload us with stress and drama.

We, as the people of God alive on the Earth today need to learn to fight back. Even if we aren't sure if a situation was caused by demonic forces, we should tell the devil to back off.

Matthew 18:18 says, *"Whatever you bind on Earth shall be bound in Heaven, and whatever you loose on Earth will be loose in Heaven."* What does that mean? It means Jesus gave us authority to bind up demonic forces that are interfering with our lives, and loose angels to work on our behalf.

Luke 10:19 says, *"Behold, I give your authority to trample on snakes and scorpions, and over all the power of the enemy, and nothing shall by any means hurt you."* We are supposed to command demonic forces to get out of our families and our lives. Yet, most Christians have never rebuked a demon in their life. Is it any wonder why the devil has been allowed to steal, kill, and destroy? We need to rise up in the spiritual authority we have been granted!

Chapter 5

Suicide Demons

In the last chapter, we covered how depression can be the result of demonic oppression. And while there can be several contributing factors for depression, I believe when it comes to suicide or homicide, demonic suggestions are always involved. Killing yourself or killing someone else is not a natural thought process. And a person wouldn't arrive at that conclusion unless they have been buffeted with thoughts of it in their mind first. True, a fit of rage can result in homicide. But premediated murder is a result of contemplation and persuasion of dark thoughts.

While it is the goal of all demons to steal, kill, and destroy, not all demons are death and suicide demons. Demons have different characteristics and traits. There are demons that cause sickness and disease (although, not all sickness and disease is caused by demons). There are anger and rage demons. There are sexual perversity demons. There are demons of fear and insecurity. There are even familiar spirit demons where they have taken on the personality and characteristics of a host human they occupied for years. Their appearance can look like that human host they occupied before the host died. What some people categorize as ghosts are really familiar spirits, which are demons.

While there are several categories of demons, I want to focus specifically on suicide demons in this chapter. I am going to be sharing four stories of suicide demons.

Fred's Suicide Spirit

When Fred's suicide took place in March of 1993, I was clueless about the spirit world. I later became somewhat of an expert in the matter and even wrote the book, *Real Stories of Angels, Demons, and the Supernatural* in 2013. However, in 1993, I was completely ignorant of the world of angels and demons.

I mentioned in the first chapter that I when Fred would talk to me about his "demons," I had too much college psychology and I didn't know he was referring to actual demons. Something happened when I read that hand-written page of lyrics from the Stephen Stills song, "4+20", that he left me in the manilla envelope. The section of the song that got my attention, read:

"Morning comes to sunrise, and I'm driven to my bed.
I see that it is empty and there's devils in my head
I embrace the many-colored beast,
I grow weary of the torment, can there be no peace?
And I find myself just wishing, that my life would simply cease."

When I read the line about embracing the many-colored beast, I had a *word of knowledge* that Fred contended with an actual suicide demon. I felt like God told me that not only were demons harassing his mind, but a specific suicide demon came to him and tried to convince him to take his life.

Prince of Peace

I think it is interesting that demons try to steal the peace of mind of the ones they torment. Years ago, in the late 90's, I was a member of Benny Hinn's choir for the crusades that were held in Southern California. After one of the services, I was about to leave, but I saw a commotion about 30 feet from where I was sitting. There were two ushers and five or six crusade attendees gathered around a woman. I was curious so I went over to see what was happening.

The woman was sitting in her chair, but she was acting like an animal, specifically a large cat, a black panther. I don't know how I could tell that she was acting like a black panther verses a lion, tiger, leopard, or cougar. For some reason, I just knew the manifestation of this demon was a black panther. If someone would say something to her, she was growl and even swat at them like her hand was a claw. The woman's face didn't change into the face of a large cat, but her mannerisms and movements definitely resembled a panther.

Obviously, a demon was manifesting through the woman. The woman had a child with her. A female usher took the child away so he wouldn't see what was happening with his mother.

There were well-meaning Christians yelling at the woman, trying to cast the demon out. One man asked her, "What is your name?"

And the demon snarled back and said, "Death."

I couldn't get very close to the woman because there were too many people trying to get the demon's attention. Different people in the group were yelling out Bible verses and talking about the blood of Jesus.

After a few minutes, the ushers either decided or were instructed to move the woman downstairs. The ushers couldn't get the woman to stand up. They tried to lift her, but she fell to her hands and knees. They tried to get her to stand a couple of times, but the woman started crawling on her hands and knees like a panther. Even the stride of her "walking" on all fours seemed very panther-like.

I decided I would follow along. As I was walking next to this woman, I started to say things to see what kind of reaction the demon would have. I found it so interesting that when I said, "Jesus is our Prince of Peace." The demon cringed in pain. That sentence caused more of a reaction in that demon than anything else that I said, or that the other people said to her when she was still in her seat. I repeated the sentence several times because it seemed to torture the demon.

It was that day that I realized that peace can actually be a spiritual weapon against the kingdom of darkness. Flowing in the peace of God weakens the attacks of the enemy. When we come to that place in life that we have done all we know to do, and then we stand in faith, with peace and faith in our hearts, it causes demons to whimper in defeat. It can also activate angels to work on our behalf if we have spoken the word of God over that situation. Peace is a position of faith.

Romans 16:20 says, *"The God of peace will crush Satan under your feet. The grace of our Lord Jesus Christ be with you."* What does *"God of peace"* mean? It means God makes peace. It means He has the ability to calm any storm, stop any attack, and clear any confusion. Any scheme of the enemy that has picked up momentum can be stopped in its tracks.

Do you remember when Jesus was asleep in the boat and a great storm arose and His disciples started to panic? They woke up Jesus and He spoke to the storm saying, "Peace, be still." (Mark 4:39) A tumultuous storm was instantly stopped when Jesus commanded peace.

Satan thrives in fear and ignorance. And when it comes to the mental torment he inflicts on people, he sends a sandstorm of confusion, anger, fear, hatred, strife, guilt, and panic. All of that sand falls to the ground, when God's peace arrives on the scene. Romans 16:20 says that peace crushes Satan. And, of course, when the sand in the sandstorm falls, it is under our feet. The devil's wiles and schemes will fall at the command of peace. The frenzied demons must stop in their tracks when "peace, be still" is spoken in authority by someone who is speaking it in faith, with a revelational understanding of what they are commanding.

Look at the second half of the Romans 16:20 verse. It says, *'the grace of our Lord Jesus Christ be with you."* When there is a grace on us to do something, that means we have a special ability to do it. I believe this verse is telling us that God will bestow a grace on us, the body of Christ, to operate in the peace of God and invoke the command of "peace" over situations that the devil is trying to wreak havoc on.

The last part of that verse says, "be with you." But the "be" is in italics in the verse which means that the word was added. So instead of reading the verse to mean that

Jesus's grace can be with us, we can interpret it like the grace of Jesus is with us.

A spirit of death isn't always in the form of an animal. In fact, based on my experiences, most of the time, they are not. They usually try to disguise themselves as part of a person's personality. However, demons in general and demons of death can have a wide range of appearances.

The Drunk Demon

A friend of mine that I have known since 2007 had a problem with alcohol. I don't like to label him as an alcoholic because I don't like identity-shaping labels. In the earlier years, his issue with alcohol was much worse than it is now. He was a binge drinker. He didn't drink every day but when he did drink, he had a hard time stopping. In the early years, he used to get drunk about once a week and he would usually call or text me when he was super drunk. That pattern continued until about 2015 or 2016. Occasionally, he will too much, but to my knowledge, it only happens a few times a year. So, he is doing much better than he used to with alcohol.

Here is the issue. When he got drunk, his suicide demon usually manifested. When he was drunk, he would text all kinds of suicidal comments. It was like a totally different person was communicating through him. He became a suicidal, confrontational, angry man. He had/has an angry, pity-partier demon in him that always used to say the same things. He keeps circling around the statement saying that nobody loves him. And that demon kept looking for ways to start arguments.

When he was sober, he was not a suicidal, confrontational, angry man. In fact, he is relatively non-confrontational, and he is emotionally balanced. He is a nice guy with a good heart. He has anxiety and a stronghold of fear in his subconscious mind. But for the most part, he is very mellow. But when he was drunk, he was wounded and desperate for love. You may think, well, "maybe that is just an aspect of his personality that he just keeps hidden when he is sober." That would be a natural assumption. However, when I was talking and texting him when he was drunk, I knew when I was talking to my drunk friend and when I was communicating with his demon. The demon used a different tone, speech pattern, and word choice than my friend. And no, he didn't have multiple personality disorder. He just had a demon that was trying to emotionally devastate and kill him.

I told my friend several times that he had a suicide demon in him that took over when he was drunk. I told him he needed deliverance, and he needed to not drink alcohol at all. I told him about his suicide demon when he was sober because he didn't listen when he was drunk. It is difficult to counsel someone when they are drunk. And it's difficult to attempt deliverance over the phone or through text messages. Usually in those situations, the best thing you can do is to command peace over the person's mind and rebuke the demon to back off. I have done that dozens of times with him and a couple of other times with other suicidal people that have called me. It won't get rid of the demon all together, but it will cause the suicide demon to back off and the person can sleep off the booze. I will talk more about casting a suicide demon out of someone in Chapter Seven.

The Green-Eyed Girl

One summer night in 1996, my friend Betty called and was bored and wanted to drive down to Laguna Beach. Neither of us had much money at the time and it seemed like a good excuse to get out of the house. After we parked, we bought hot chocolates. We were about to walk around the shops, but we noticed that something was going on across the street at the beach.

As we walked across the street, we noticed that there were percussionists playing instruments with an audience of about 50 people. There were also five or six people dancing. The musicians were on the benches facing the ocean. The dancers and the audience were facing the musicians in a semi-circle. After Betty and I walked up, we stood under a tree about 20 feet from the benches where the musicians were playing. I think we were the only spectators behind the musicians and everyone else was in front of them.

After a couple of minutes, Betty said, "Do you see that?" I looked around and saw what Betty was referring to. There was a girl dancing, who appeared to be around

20 years old with a demon manifesting through her. Her head was shaved before that became a trend and her eyeballs were glowing neon green. We didn't see her pupils. We only saw the whites of her eyes but instead of white, they were glowing neon green. My assumption was her eyes were rolled back in her head and that was why we didn't see pupils. The girl was facing the drummers so that was probably the reason why the crowd didn't notice her eyes.

When I saw the girl, I told Betty, "Now we know why we are here." We started praying in the spirit for the girl. Soon after we started praying for her, one of the percussionists stood up, and turned around and started staring at me and Betty. He was playing a cow bell and he appeared to be trying to block our view of the girl. Now, bear in mind, it was loud. There was no way anyone there could have heard me and Betty praying.

I told Betty we should target the girl from two different angles, so I moved about 20 feet to the right. Betty stayed under the tree, and I stood under a streetlamp. The guy with the cow bell couldn't block both of us, so he adjusted himself to try to block my view.

At that point, another musician who was sitting on the bench, turn his head around and started staring at me. He was smiling at me. But it wasn't a *hey baby, I think you're cute* smile. It was a *I know what you're doing* smile.

It was obvious to me that demons were manifesting out of the two musicians that were staring at me. In fact,

I felt like I had a word of knowledge that there were more than 100 demons there that night. It was a demon party and demons like to party.

An indignation rose in me, and I decreed, "Just as this streetlight illuminates this dark place, so the Holy Spirit illuminates this dark place. When light comes, darkness must flee. I command every demon in this place to go in Jesus' name!" Even though I said it out loud, the music was so loud, the people didn't hear me, but the spirit world heard me.

Suddenly, the music stopped, and everyone started to leave. The girl with the neon green eyes started to walk away and before I knew it, I was running towards her and yelling at her to stop. She turned around and burst into tears. By the time I reached her, tears were running down her cheeks. Through her hysterical crying, she said, "You don't understand. You don't understand. When I turned around, I didn't see you. I saw Jesus coming towards me."

I told her there was a demon manifesting through her when she was dancing, and I wanted to cast it out of her. She quickly agreed. By that time, Betty and the girl's sister were gathered around as well. I then had a word of knowledge. I said, "There's also a demon that torments you at night. That demon must go too. I'm going to command these demons to leave but you need to accept Jesus in our heart."

She burst out into tears all over again and asked, "How did you know? How did you know?" She went on to say that for the last two weeks, a black demon had appeared to her in her bedroom every night. It told her what a terrible person she was and told her to kill herself. She said she had been sleeping in her sister's room because she was so terrified of it.

I commanded the demons to leave and led her in a prayer of salvation. I gave her a track so she would have the Bible verses for the salvation prayer. I suggested she start attending the church that had its info on the back of that track. I also told her she should talk to someone on the pastoral team and tell them what happened.

As Betty and I were in the car driving, we saw the musicians down a small back alley. They were playing their percussion instruments, but there weren't any dancers or spectators with them. They lost their audience. The sight of them made me laugh. When I had commanded the demons to leave, I didn't mean that the demons had to take their human hosts with them. With all the activity of ministering to the girl, it hadn't dawned on me that the demon dance party concert had ended right after I commanded the demons to go. But, because several of the demons were in people, that meant that the people had to leave.

I mention this experience because the demon of suicide in this case wasn't one that had attached itself to girl's soul. The suicide demon chose to appear to her to scare and bully her. Of course, the girl did have a demon in her and that is why her eyes were neon green.

Summary

The four different experiences referenced in this chapter show some of the ways suicide demons can manifest. It can have the appearance of a many-colored beast that the Stephen Stills song mentions. It can manifest as a dark, evil, brooding entity residing in a person as demonstrated by the black panther spirit of death. It can manifest as an over-emotional, angry, wounded spirit that masquerades as an aspect of a person's personality as it did in my friend. Or it can be an external demon that comes to torment a person, as it did would the girl with the neon green eyes.

Their appearance can vary quite a bit. But the most common way a suicide demon will attack a person is with subtle suggestions they whisper to a person making them think it is just their own negative self-talk. Demons prefer to hide. When they hide, there is less chance of being cast out. So, they will try to impersonate a person's thoughts.

Chapter 6

A Suicidal Friend

If you have ever been on the phone with a suicidal friend or family member, you know you need wisdom to handle the situation. You try to gauge the mental state of your loved one. Are they just talking, or have they planned out a means to take their life? Is this a cry for help where you just need to counsel them, or should you call the police so they can issue a 3-day 5150 hold? (A 5150 hold is a California law where an officer or clinician can place a person on an involuntary psychiatric hold if they deem the person is a danger to themselves or others.)

Hopefully you are able to help them in the beginning stages of their suicidal thoughts before they reach the point of having a gun, knife, razorblade, rope, or pills in their hands. You may feel unqualified to handle the situation but believe it or not, there is a lot you can do to help them.

(The advice given in this section assumes that you, as a friend or family member of the suicidal person, are a Christian. The suicidal person may not have a relationship with God, but the input given in this chapter is geared towards you being a Christian.)

Offer Hope

Even though a suicidal person may be under a mental attack by a demon, I wouldn't address that at the beginning of the conversation. The demon has told the person that their situation is hopeless. I would try to infuse hope back into them because their supply has been depleted. It's like when some has been stabbed and they are losing blood. Emergency medical personnel will administer an IV of either saline or blood, so the patient's blood pressure doesn't get too low. Speaking encouraging, hope-filled words can be the IV they desperately need before anything else.

What causes depression and suicide? The simple answer is hopelessness and despair. A person gets to a point that they either believe their situation won't improve or they have simply given up on everything. There are usually feeling deep sadness and emotional pain. Yes, a person can be hard-wired with a bent towards discouragement, their brain chemicals can be out of whack, or they could be going through terrible circumstances in life. All these things have a bearing. But ultimately, a suicidal person feels hopeless.

We covered some of the factors that can lead a person into discouragement. Their personality type, soul iniquities, and nudge factors can influence their pull towards depression. It may be a good idea to examine those factors and see which ones may apply to your suicidal friend. If you know what the areas of weakness are, you will know more how to target your words of encouragement.

It was mentioned earlier in the book that most situations are like diamonds. They are multi-faceted. There are details and variables that your suicidal friend is not considering. Your friend has, most likely, magnified one side or aspect of their situation and made it a huge wall that they can't get around. Well, offering them different perspectives so they can view the situation from different angles, can significantly help their vantage point. It can help them see the situation isn't as hopeless as they think it is.

Love Them

In addition to feeling hopeless, many of those that battle suicidal thoughts, feel like nobody loves them. Look at the drunk demon story from the last chapter. That demon tortured the man trying to convince him that nobody loved him. The girl with the neon green eyes said that the demon that visited her at night told her what a terrible person she was. Well, in essence that was telling her she was unlovable.

If a person is feeling discouraged and they happen to come to mind, take an action. Send them a text to cheer them up. Pray that ministering angels will come and encourage them. Pray that God will send other people across their path to brighten their day. Send them a gift that will remind them that somebody cares. Message them a funny video. There is no harm that can come from reaching out and extending human kindness and love towards those close to you.

Refuse the urge to keep score. Don't rationalize, "I have texted them three times and they haven't reached out to me once." It's not a competition. You may not be the one who needs the extra encouragement right now. Be sensitive to the Holy Spirit's leading and not the scoreboard.

Everyone has positive and negative aspects to their personality. We all have strengths and weaknesses. When we think about our suicidal friend, try to see them through the eyes of God. Don't focus on their weaknesses. See their positive qualities. See what makes them unique and special.

Philippians 4:8 says, *"Finally, brethren, whatever things are true, whatever things are noble, whatever things are just, whatever things are pure, whatever things are lovely, whatever things are of a good report, if there is any virtue and if there is anything praiseworthy – meditate on these things."*

When we focus on the good in them, then the love of God can shine through us to them more. We aren't faking our concern because we don't want them to be discouraged. We genuinely want to help them get out of the pit of despair. When we focus on their positive traits, it will be easier to encourage them and help them see the positive. When they are in the snare of depression, they can't see the good in themselves. God wants us to remind them.

Invite Them Out

When a person is discouraged and depressed, they usually isolate themselves. However, even if that is the case, don't stop inviting them to hang out together. Invite them to lunch or to join you at a Bible Study or other social event. Letting them know you value them and want their company can do more good than you can imagine. The demon has probably convinced them that they are unlovable, people tolerate them, but don't really like them and value them. That lie can easily be broken but extending invitations.

Invite them to do something in nature. If you live near the ocean or a lake, set up an outing to see and even feel nature. Walk barefoot on sand or on grass. Watch a sunset. Visiting nature can do wonders for the soul.

Volunteer

Volunteer for something and invite your discouraged friend to join you. Giving your time and energy to a good cause can break discouragement off a person. When someone is depressed, their attention is turned inward, and they are focusing on what is wrong with them and what is wrong in their life. Volunteering to help others who is less fortunate, helps us count our blessings, and it helps us feel good about ourselves. Volunteer at a soup kitchen, homeless shelter, convalescent home, VA hospital, or animal rescue. Find a cause that touches your heart and do good.

Invite Them to Church

There have been a few times where I have brought a person to church, and God used the pastor to specifically talk about an issue or question that was on the mind of the visitor. One time I brought a visitor to a Sunday night service and when the service ended, he just sat there in his chair stunned. He didn't get up to leave. He sat there in amazement because the pastor told a story about a fishing experience and that story made the visitor know that God orchestrated the service just to speak to him. Apparently, there were details of the story that were very significance to the visitor.

Another Sunday evening, I brought my brother Ken to church. The same thing happened with him. He sat there stunned that God had the pastor talk about things that were meant for my brother Ken to hear. On the car ride over, Ken brought up three or four topics that bugged him about Christians and church. The pastor talked about each one of them and answered his questions. Ken knew that it wasn't a manmade setup. He was with me the entire time. He knew I couldn't have snuck off and called or had a private conversation to give the details of the conversation in the car. Even though there were hundreds in attendance at that service, it made Ken feel loved by God that God would care enough to have the pastor address his questions.

Oftentimes, when a visitor comes and just soaks up the atmosphere, the Holy Spirit will minister to them directly. They may find themself crying for no reason during praise and worship. Or they may feel the presence of God in the sanctuary. A greeter can smile at them in such a way that makes them feel sincerely welcomed. Church services offer multiple ways that God can reach a person, so it is a good idea to get your depressed friend to church.

Increase Discernment

I mentioned in Chapter Three that when I received the Baptism of the Holy Spirit with the evidence of speaking in tongues, it greatly increased my ability to hear from God. If you haven't received the baptism of the spirit or it has been dormant for a while, I encourage you to receive it or reactivate it.

When you are speaking to your suicidal friend, you need to hear from God on what to say and how to say it. If you are on the phone with them, it is most likely by divine design. It is probably God's intent to use you to help them. The more spiritually in tune you are, the more effective you will be.

There are definite benefits to receiving the baptism of the Spirit.

1) Gives us Power

Acts 1:8 says, *"But you shall receive power when the Holy Spirit has come upon you and you shall be witnesses of Me in Jerusalem, and in all Judea and Samaria, and to the ends of the earth."* Jude 20 says, *"But you beloved, building yourself up on your most holy faith, praying in the Holy Spirit."* Praying in tongues builds you up and makes you stronger spiritually. When your spirit-man is strengthened, you become more of a powerhouse for God. Your faith has teeth. Praying in tongues strengthens your faith and when your faith is strong, mountains can move.

2) Gives us Knowledge

Praying in tongues also opens an avenue where God can speak wisdom, knowledge, and understanding to us more clearly. John 14:26 says, *"But the Helper, the Holy Spirit, whom the Father will send in My name, He will teach you all things, and bring to your remembrance all things that I said to you."* God wants His people to have wisdom and under-standing. After you have the baptism of the Holy Spirit, the Spirit of God becomes easier to recognize. The Bible says in John 10:27, *"My sheep hear My voice."* Well, God's voice of correction, direction, and affection becomes easier to recognize as you seek God and study His word after you have received the baptism of the Holy Spirit.

3) We Pray God's Will

Tongues may sound strange to those that haven't experienced the baptism of the Holy Spirit and it may even make them feel a little uncomfortable. But when we pray in tongues, we are not doing it for the entertainment or approval of others. When we pray in tongues, we are praying to God and God understands what we are saying. 1 Corinthians 14:2 says, *"For he who speaks in a tongue does not speak to men but to God, for no one understands him; however, in the spirit he speaks mysteries."* Not only does God understand our prayers, He is the One praying His will through us. Romans 8:26-27 says, *"Likewise the Spirit also helps in our weaknesses. For we do not know what we should pray for as we ought but the Spirit Himself makes intercession for us with groaning which cannot be uttered. Now He who searches the hearts knows what the mind of the Spirit is, because He makes intercession for the saints according to the will of God."*

When I have been on the phone with a suicidal person, there have been times I have mentioned that a demon is whispering in their ear, and other times I haven't mentioned the demonic suggestions. I allow the Holy Spirit to guide me with each call. There isn't a boilerplate routine for counseling a suicidal person. That is why we need to hear from the Holy Spirit in real time. To date, I haven't prayed in tongues while I was on the phone with the suicidal person, although I am open to doing it. Normally, after I hang up the phone, I will pray in tongues and in English for the suicidal person. I will command that the demons stop harassing their mind and quote scriptures to them. I speak peace to their mind and emotions. After I finish praying for them, I get quiet and ask God if there is anything else I need to do. I will usually continue to pray for them until I sense that they are okay.

The demonic suggestions will typically subside. I usually don't try to do a full deliverance over the phone because that demon can just have the host hang up the phone. Deliverance is usually an in-person thing and its best to do it with two or three other strong Christians in the room with you.

If you do attempt deliverance, it is ideal for the person with the demon to have some spiritual understanding. Perhaps give them a quick lesson before or after you cast the demon out of them. Remember, demons get invited in when we agree with their suggestions. If the person doesn't know how to keep the screen door shut with their thought life, they can unknowingly invite the demon back in by their agreement with the demonic suggestions.

(If you want information on how to receive the Baptism of the Holy Spirit, there is an article on my website that explains it. Visit www.DeborahDelbridge.com, and read the article entitled the Baptism of the Holy Spirit.)

Spiritual Teeth

What made one hundred demons obey me when I commanded them to leave in the green-eyed girl experience at Laguna Beach? Was I born with extra faith potential or an extra measure of spiritual authority? No. My spiritual authority potential was the same as every believer's authority potential.

The reason those demons had to obey me was, a few months before that confrontation, I had had a revelation of what I commanded that night. I had faith in what I was saying. The truth of the statement, "When light comes, darkness must flee," had dropped down from head knowledge to my subconscious mind. I had faith. I believed what I was commanding.

By that time in my life, I had encountered angels and demons. No one had to convince me that the spirit world was real. With my natural eyes, I had seen angels and demons.

A few months before the Laguna Beach outing, I remember I had contemplated the whole *when light comes* thing. I had already been equating demons with cockroaches. In my mind, I imagined a kitchen that had a cockroach problem. When a person would go to the kitchen at night and flip on the light switch, the cockroaches would run and hide. Cockroaches like to hide. Demons like to hide. Demons operate in fear and ignorance. When they are exposed, they often try to hide.

In additional to envisioning cockroaches running away when the light is turn on, I also remember staring at my light switch in my bedroom. When a light is turned on, the dark can't stay. Darkness doesn't have a choice. I remember thinking, when light comes, darkness must go. Then I thought about the John 8:12 scripture that says, *"Then Jesus spoke to them again saying, "I am the light of the world. He who follows Me shall not walk in darkness but have the light of life."* Jesus is the light. We have Jesus in our heart. We carry the light. We have the authority to bring light into dark places.

I encourage you to think about both the *demons are cockroaches* thing and the *power of light to drive away darkness* thing. Meditate and rehearse them in your mind until the revelation drops down into your gut. Viewing demons as cockroaches is important. I think most people give demons too much power by how they view them. Humans have been conditioned to fear evil. We, as a society, have seen too many horror movies and suspenseful videos. We have been conditioned to fear anything evil. We give demons power when we fear them. Sure, demons have power over non-believers and ignorant Christians. But they don't have power over the Christians that understand their spiritual authority.

How do you have faith (belief in your subconscious mind) to command demons to go? Rehearse the scriptures that tell us our authority. Listen to preaching videos on the subject. Educate yourself and make an effort to get authority faith in your gut. Faith comes by hearing and hearing by the word of God as it says in Romans 10:17 so allow your ears to hear verses and teaching on the subject. Read Kenneth Hagin's book, *The Believer's Authority*. Even incorporate daily affirmations of saying, "God's light dwells in me. Darkness must flee from me."

Then, do the same thing with the *"Peace, be still,"* command. Jesus commanded it, that gives us the authority to command it. Do a word study on the word *peace*. Peace means wholeness and completeness. It means the absence of struggle, strife, conflict, or noise. The word *Shalom* is a salutation in the Jewish community that means *peace*. In the Jewish translation of Shalom/Peace, it encompasses soundness, health, safety, prosperity, and it carries with it the implication of permanence.

When we command *peace* over a situation and we understand what we are saying, we are rebuking the *Lord of the Flies*, Beelzebub, the kingdom of darkness, to stop their attacks.

Matthew 5:9 says, *"Blessed are the peacemakers, for they shall be called sons of God."* It doesn't say peacekeepers. God is not telling us to just stand there and do nothing. He isn't telling us not to engage in strife and drama. He is telling us to be peacemakers. Jesus is telling us to make the atmosphere peaceful by His authority. The verse even says that is how people will recognize that we are children of God, if we make or command peace. People will call us *sons of God,* when we do what Jesus did when He was here. He commanded peace, and we need to start commanding peace over situations and people.

With both of these commands, *"Darkness must flee"* and *"Peace, be still,"* it isn't about the words. It's about faith in those words. Get a revelation of the authority that God has given you and wants you to use. Get that revelation down in your gut. When you get it, when you know it, it won't just help your prayers for your suicidal friends, it will exponentially cause dramatic change in your life. You will be equipped with spiritual teeth in the spirit realm.

Chapter 7

Are You Depressed?

If you struggle with depression, please know that just because you feel that way today, doesn't mean you will feel that way tomorrow. Change is absolutely possible. Also, please don't feel embarrassed or ashamed. People can have physical sicknesses, diseases, injuries, or ailments and they are not scorned. Yet, for some reason, if a person doesn't feel *hunky dory*, they are perceived as deficient.

Besides, with what has been happening in the world the last few years, a very high percentage of people are discouraged and depressed. With the pandemic lockdowns, economic losses, supply chain shortages, inflation, and the heartbreaking deaths of our loved ones, multiples of people are in an emotional pit.

As we walk through this chapter, I encourage you to keep an open mind. I'm going to address several variables. Before you quickly rule something out and assume it doesn't apply to you, please consider it with an open mind. Most of us think we are self-aware, but we often have blind spots and areas of ignorance.

Brain Chemicals

We talked about brain chemicals earlier in the book, but I want to cover some other aspects of them in this section. Do you think your brain chemicals are out of whack? Do you think your dopamine and serotonin levels are low? For decades, psychiatrists have prescribed medications to patients that they feel have low levels of happy brain chemicals.

However, there are recent studies that are changing the way some doctors approach the topic. Dopamine is important. It is a neurotransmitter. It is highly involved in our reward center. If our dopamine level is low, we can become susceptible to depression and Parkinson's disease. The downside is when people take medications to treat their low dopamine, the effectiveness of the drugs wear off.

Some doctors are encouraging their patients to do things that would allow their bodies to produce it naturally. Scientists used to think that dopamine was made in our nerves and adrenal glands but now they are saying it is made in our G.I. tract. Some doctors are encouraging their patients to take probiotics so the right kinds of bacteria can help with the production of dopamine. So apparently, good gut health improves our mental health.

Exercise can help produce happy brain chemicals as well. Endorphins and dopamine are manufactured when we exercise. So, in addition to exercise helping our metabolism and circulation and helping us fight off strokes, heart disease, and diabetes, it also produces dopamine.

Laughter can also alter dopamine and serotonin activity. The endorphins that are released during laughter can help when a person is depressed or feels uncomfortable. So, if you are feeling down, watch funny videos. It isn't a waste of time; it helps our brain chemicals balance out.

Sometimes, the problem isn't the amount of dopamine a person has. Sometimes, the issue is a problem with our receptors in our brain. Dopamine cross over our synapses and jumps from a cell to a receptor. We can have a low electrical potential which means the dopamine can't make it across our synapses. The same is true for serotonin; sometimes, it can't cross over the synapse. There is a device that has been approved by the FDA that helps raise the electrical potential in the brain.

It's called a Fisher Wallace stimulator and it can be very beneficial for people with low electrical activity.

A new study that has come out from University College in London states that there is no evidence that depression is caused by low brain chemicals. They suggest the underpinning that led to millions of Americans being placed on anti-depressants can be completely wrong. They found stronger evidence that stress and trauma have a greater likelihood of causing depression. They suggest that taking anti-depressants are worse than not taking them because anti-depressants have the side effect of causing suicidal thoughts.

In light of the new study, it may be a good idea to incorporate some of the natural ways of increasing dopamine and then seek an answer from God to see if you should take medications. Personally, I am neither for or against antidepressants and other brain chemical medications. When considering medications, it is best to evaluate them on a case-by-case basis. They may be the right solution for one person but not for another.

Let's not overlook a big takeaway from the study. The study showed stress caused depression. Well, most of us knew that. It was stated earlier in the book that the more we mediate on negative thoughts and rehearse them in our minds, the easier it is to go from discouragement into depression. What we think about and talk about absolutely affects our mood, and our negative thoughts can lower our positive brain chemicals. Usually, we can control our discouragement and depression by what we choose to think about and what thoughts we allow to run rampant in our imagination.

Our Personality

It was mentioned in Chapter Two that there are factors in our genetics that influence the likelihood of us falling into depression. Personality types, soul iniquities, and generational curses were mentioned. Certainly, having a melancholy personality dramatically increases the potential for depression. Melancholy people feel emotions deeper than other personality types. The feel love, betrayal, and sadness stronger than others, which makes them more prone to depression because they can get more emotionally wounded.

Every personality trait is like a coin. There is a good side to it and a bad side. That characteristic can be used to do good, or it can be a self-sabotaging force in our life. We don't get a free pass for bad habits, sin, and self-sabotaging behavior just because a specific behavior pattern comes easy for us. A man with an issue of lust doesn't get a free pass to cheat on his wife. Likewise, a person with a melancholy personality doesn't get a free pass to hold on to unforgiveness. We all have strengths and weaknesses, and God has called us to conquer our weakness by the grace He gives us.

Soul Iniquities

Diseases of the soul have been discussed already in this book, but I want to reiterate some things. Chapter three described soul iniquities as cancers of the soul that can go undetected for years and can destroy relationships, careers, and even destinies. Soul iniquities aren't always the root cause of depression, but they can be the cause. There are a few soul iniquities that can lead to depression or, at a minimum, influence the pull discouragement may have on us.

It is also important to recognize that there can be mixture. There can be a soul iniquity influencing discouragement at the same time emotional wounds are causing significant pain. It isn't one or the other. In fact, in most cases, there is the presence of both, the pain of an event or loss and the existence of an underlying soul iniquity.

Pride is the first soul iniquity and the most difficult to detect in ourselves. Everyone has pride and there are traces of pride in the other *diseases of the soul.* Some people have a huge festering root of pride, while other people have less of it because they tether their thoughts and actions. Pride leads to deceptive thinking and the more pride a person has, the more delusional their thinking can be. Pride makes us think that our version of reality is truth, when, in fact, our view of reality is just a summary of our opinions. The more pride we have, the less in touch with true reality we are. I don't mean to sound too harsh, especially if you are feeling discouraged and depressed. But it is important for us to realize that our outlook, our version of truth, isn't the full scoop of any situation. We can believe a false reality.

Pride, in addition to leading to deceptive thinking, has us always focused on ourselves. When we are looking at ourselves and rehearsing what our needs and desires are, we tend to overemphasize what we perceive to be wrong in our lives. When all our thoughts are on self, self, self – then, they aren't on God or other people. Pride causes us to get selfish and self-centered. There will always be situations in our lives that are not ideal. But if we take the focus off of ourselves, and put it on God, He will lift our gaze and give us a new prospective.

There is a well-known principle that if someone is depressed, they should help others and that will cause their depression to lift. Helping those that are less fortunate can break up our obsession with what we don't like in our own lives. Helping others enriches our souls. There is an intrinsic satisfaction that comes from doing good and making the world a better place. Helping other people and focusing on their needs can help lift us out of our discouragement funk.

Another *disease of the soul* that causes depression is having a negative, critical, and judgmental spirit. When people have this soul iniquity, they only think about and rehearse negative things. I used to know someone that had this. Boy, he wore me out. Literally, everything he thought about it and every word out of his mouth was negative. It was exhausting being in the same room as him. He thought everybody and everything was bad. He criticized everything. Well, of course, a person can get depressed if all they think about and rehearse in their mind is negative. It would be easy to embrace hopelessness with that kind of outlook.

Occasionally, a stronghold of jealousy in a person's subconscious can cause them to get discouraged and lead to depression. Because jealous people are constantly comparing themselves to other people, they tend to focus on what they don't have.

A stronghold of fear in a person's subconscious mind can certainly manifest as anxiety. When a person has anxiety, they typically rehearse negative fears in their mind over and over. They just keep circling and playing the same record over and over in their mind. They have no peace. They can turn a small speedbump into a mountain in their imagination. They can get to a negative mental place where they won't allow themselves to see any alternative except to take their life.

Diseases of the soul require both repentance and behavioral changes which are addressed in my book, *Blind Spots and Wrinkles*. Am I saying that discouragement and depression can be rooted in sin? Yes, that is what I am saying. A person can have deep emotional wounds and there can be other causes, of course, but our unrenewed Adamic nature can certainly be at the root of our depression.

Relationship with God

The most important factor in getting rid of depression and improving your quality of life is to focus on improving your relationship with God. If you're not a Christian, you need to surrender your life to God. If you are a Christian, you need to seek God, so you have a more intimate relationship with Him. Study the Bible. Watch good, Spirit-filled preaching and teaching online. Attend a good church. Seek God for the Baptism of the Holy Spirit with the evidence of speaking in other tongues. Develop your spiritual language and pray in tongues every day. Be careful what you listen to. Don't listen to evil or sinful music or videos. Be careful what you allow your ears to hear and your eyes to see.

The goal is to get to that place in your Christian walk where you can talk to God, and you can hear God speak to you. That is possible and it is the kind of close relationship that God wants to have with us. We can develop our discernment, so we know the direction and purpose for our lives. We can get God's correction, direction, and affection if we learn to hear His voice.

I'm convinced that a person that truly hears from God can't be depressed. Depression happens when people feel hopeless. Well, if God is communicating with you, you won't feel hopeless. You won't feel lonely if the God of the Universe is your friend. You won't carry emotional wounds, when you are close with the Healer. Developing your relationship with God will help you conquer depression.

Deliverance

In the last chapter that gave advise to those that were trying to help depressed and suicidal friends and family, I didn't encourage them to attempt deliverance over the phone. I mentioned that they can rebuke a demon, but it will probably come back if the suicidal person doesn't know how to chaperon their own thoughts. We need to train ourselves to not to agree with negative thoughts because those negative thoughts can be demonic suggestions. And if we agree with demonic suggestions, it invites demons to take residence in our soul. Remember, the spirit world operates by agreement.

Most people are not sure how to "take every thought captive," as the Bible says in 2 Cor. 10:5. It's simple; pay attention to your thoughts. Call out and call down the negative ones. Replace the negative thought with a positive affirmation. If paying attention to your thoughts is new to you, you may want to keep a journey so you can write down the thoughts that are going through your mind. Once on paper, you can read them back and determine which thoughts are of God, demonic suggestion, or your own imagination. Once you get in the practice of it, it will become much easier to pay attention to the random thoughts that cross your mind.

Once you feel like you know how to do it, you can go to a church that practices deliverance, or you can do it yourself. You don't have to make it a big deal. You can command the demon to leave you. Demons like to hide so it may pretend to go but if you are still getting harassed by it, then you know it is back. You can ask God for discernment so you can recognize when "thoughts" are yours and which ones are demonic suggestions.

Depression-Breaking Actions

This next section will review some actions you can take to dig yourself out of a discouragement pit.

Exercise

It was mentioned before that exercise releases happy brain chemicals and its true. We feel better about ourselves after exercise. We feel like we are controlling our body, not our body controlling us. Our flesh nature wants food, comfort, and laziness. But exercise makes us feel empowered, and it boosts our self-esteem.

Hygiene

Often times when we are discouraged, we don't want to get out of bed. If we don't have to go to work or school, we may just lay in bed all day and not do anything. Hygiene routines of showering, washing your hair, shaving, brushing your hair, putting on makeup, and getting dressed may all wane when we are depressed. But doing these grooming practices can actually help fight discouragement. When we do things that make us feel at our best, it changes our mood. Our self-esteem will be stronger, and we will feel better about ourselves if we keep up the grooming routine.

Community

God created us to be social beings. We are not meant to be alone and isolated. But in today's society, it is easy to disconnect and not interact with other people. We used to be good friends with our co-workers. Now, many industries have switched to working from home. We used to talk to people when we shopped. Now we can have everything delivered. We used to befriend other students. Now we remote learn online. In our advancements of convenience, we have made it easier to isolate from other people.

It is emotionally healthy to have a sense of community. Recently, I was chatting with a dog owner at the dog park. She was a singer and she had been hired to perform at a retreat for a men's mountain biking club. She said the men talked about how the bike club not only helped their physical health but helped their emotional well-being. She said there were a couple of them that said they had been depressed and suicidal before joining the men's mountain biking club. They testified that they felt the club saved their life.

Having a sense of community and a sense of belonging can be very healing for the soul. Belonging to a community meets an intrinsic desire to be included and valued.

What are your interests and hobbies? Consider joining a community of others that enjoy the same hobby. Is there a sport you like? Consider joining a league for that sport. Do you have a dog? If so, start taking your dog to the dog park every morning. Can you sing? Join the choir at church. Even if you are shy, challenge yourself to join groups of others that share the same interests.

Your Job

If you don't have a job, get a job. If your job isn't rewarding or you work in a repressive atmosphere, look for a new job. Enjoying what you do for a living is important for mental health. Your quality of life is too important to work at a job you hate. If you are afraid of making a move, seek godly counsel and allow them to help you weigh out your options.

As you read in this book, my friendship with Sharon, who I met at work, changed my life. She didn't change my personality, but rather, her confidence rubbed off on me, and it allowed my own personality to shine through. I had been in a depression after the breakup with my first long term boyfriend and hanging out with Sharon snapped me out of it.

Some of your dearest and closest friendships can start by befriending the people you work with. Don't underestimate the value that your job can provide you. It isn't just a paycheck. It's an opportunity to learn and perfect a craft and it's a place to cultivate relationships.

Get a Pet

If your living situation allows you to have a pet, I would strongly recommend it. A dog or cat can give you unconditional love and fill a void that you didn't know you had.

As of this writing, I have a dog and four cats. All of them want my attention. My cat, Grayson, is very affectionate and *lovey dovey*. If it were up to him, he would spend all of his time laying on me or trying to snuggle with my face. My nine-month-old puppy, Oliver, is extremely jealous and believes all my attention should be on him. The competition between them for vying for my attention is comical at times. If I'm sitting up in my bed working on the computer, Grayson will come and lay across my chest making it extremely difficult to see my computer screen. Then, not to be outdone, Oliver will wedge himself between my face and Grayson, in essence, pushing Grayson away. If I am on the computer and won't let the animals lay on me, Grayson will come and lay to my side so his head is on my shoulder. He will do anything to get close to my face. When Oliver sees that, he will come lay his head on my other shoulder. Or if the jealousy is too much for him, he will try to bug Grayson, so Grayson moves.

Not only can pets give you more love and affection than you want, but they are also loyal to their humans. They desire to be with their human, and they let you know when they have missed you. Other people may pet-sit while you are away, but your pet will let you know that no one can take your place.

The responsibility of caring for a pet is good for you. Pets get you up early so you can't lay in bed all morning. Having the responsibility for caring for a pet has kept many people from following through with their suicidal thoughts. They don't want their pet orphaned, so they resist the negative voice that tells them to end their life.

Get Involved at Church

I would highly recommend getting involved at a church. The sense of community within a church can be much stronger than with other community groups. Church groups can feel like family. There is often a level of love, kindness, and charity that other non-Christian community programs can't compare with. I have known several people that have said they feel closer to their church family than they do towards their biological family. Church friends not only provide friendship, but they can also give you spiritual guidance and counsel.

Closing Thoughts

I want to encourage you to recognize that you are more powerful than you think you are. Your potential is bigger than you think it is. You are not a victim. Don't let your emotions and your demons lie to you. Recognize that the Holy Spirit in you can link arms with your faith and conquer any mountain. Your problems are not bigger than God. The Holy Spirit will help you navigate your way through the mess and cause you to be victorious over the obstacles.

When you read your Bible, go to church, listen to preaching and teaching videos, and talk to God, it opens the communication channel for God to speak to you. All it takes is a Rhema word (spoken word) from God to drop down into your heart, and you can change the world.

God chose that you would be born in this time in history. He has specific assignments for you. You are special. You have a purpose. You may not have discovered it yet, but there are specific things God has called and ordained that you would do. Lift your head. See the forest through the trees. Wipe off the mud so you can run your race.

Chapter 8

Emotional Healing

This book has addressed several topics so far. I have touched on what traditional psychology says the causes of depression are. I have taught on our subconscious mind and how our beliefs and behaviors are driven from there. I have addressed why some people may be more likely to be challenged with depression based on their personality, soul iniquities, as well as other nudge factors. I have talked about the role that demonic forces play in depression and suicide. And I have given advice to the depressed person as well as to the Christian friend that is trying to help them.

The area that I haven't covered very well is emotional healing. Yes, it was communicated that getting close to God can heal our emotions and that is very true. But I want to go a little deeper in this chapter. I also want to share some experiences that demonstrate that God wants to bring emotional healing to hurting people.

Wounds and Walls

While we understand that our depression can be rooted in our personality, our soul iniquities, and other traumas in our life, we also understand that we are still left with a wounded heart. Whatever the original cause may be, it doesn't change the fact that we may still have a broken heart from the disappointments and tragedies in our lives.

If we have an emotional wound that has healed, that doesn't mean we won't get wounded again in the future. New situations arise and we can experience betrayal, rejection, or failure all over again. Most of us have emotional scars from wounds that have healed correctly but that doesn't mean that we don't also have scabs of emotional wounds that are in the process of healing.

When we have a physical wound, we usually clean it and bandage it. We protect it. That is good and that is expected. We don't put a bandage on a healed scar. We don't try to cover and protect it if it is truly healed.

A sign that a wound has an infection or didn't heal correctly is, we are still protecting it. We are still treating it like a painful injury. We may think it is healed. But if we continue to put up walls of protection around our heart so we can't get hurt again, then the injury hasn't healed properly. We may not even realize that we have a bandage on that old injury. We may have erected a wall of protection around it and my not even know. We don't talk about it or let people see it. A permanent wall of protection is built around our heart, and we unknowingly keep people out.

We may not understand why we feel lonely or don't have close friends. We may not realize that we are one that keeps others away. That major emotional wound that we thought was healed, may cause us to not let others get too close.

There are others of us that are contending with minor wounds. They aren't critical, but they are still painful. We may have a smile on our face and look healed and whole, but inwardly, we know we aren't. We know we have some injuries, but we choose to keep them private. I am talking about the stuff that husbands and wives don't tell each other. I'm talking about little injuries that our best friend doesn't even know about. We put up walls. We hide them and protect them. Afterall, they aren't other people's business.

A large percentage of people we see and know are deeply wounded emotionally. It's not an unforgiveness thing. They are just brokenhearted. They have gone through so much disappointment that they are broken inside. They have put up walls.

Is it any wonder why depressed people tend to isolate themselves? They put up distance walls with other people, while those with non-life-threatening wounds just put-up emotional walls. Most everyone we know walks around with emotional walls up because they are carrying emotional wounds.

Clean It

When we have a scratched knee, we know that we need to clean the wound before we put a bandage on it. We need to run water over it to rinse off any lose gravel. We may need tweezers to pick out any sand that didn't come off when we rinsed it off. We then need to put an antibiotic cream on it to prevent infection. Then, it is ready for the bandage.

The problem with most emotional wounds is people are quick to put a bandage on, meaning cover it up and protect it before they clean it. There are things we go through that we need to emotionally process. We need to *peel the onion* and sometimes ask ourselves difficult questions. There are things we can do to make sure our emotional wounds don't get infected.

1) Run water over it to rinse it. Ephesians 5:26 says, *"that He might sanctify and cleanse her by the washing of the word."* This verse is talking about the end-time church (the bride of Christ) and how we need to get

rid of our spots and wrinkles. It is saying we can get cleansed by the washing of the word. In other words, when we read our Bible and mediate on scriptures that pertain to our situation, sanctification and healing can come to our soul. The Bible is that water that we wash over our wounds.

2) Next, we get our spiritual tweezers. We need to examine our wound and pick out the stuff that doesn't belong. When we are wounded, we need to resist the tendency to blame the other person. We need to ask ourselves what role we played in the drama, and we shouldn't let a victim mindset take hold. Those tweezers are needed to pick out the gravel of assumptions and wrong conclusions. Review the incident carefully and pick out details that have any assumptions attached to them.

3) Think about that diamond thing I keep mentioning. Every situation is multifaceted and has several sides. Brainstorm and journalize possible details that you may have overlooked. Try to see the situation through the eyes of the others that are involved. Are there fears they may have that may have driven their actions or reactions? Are there other factors or concerns that affect matter? It has been my experience that *playing the devil's advocate* helps us see the situation through different filters and biases. When we can see the offense from different angles, it often takes the sting out of the emotional injury.

4) With a skinned knee, we should apply an antibiotic ointment after we have cleaned it. We need to do the same spiritually. In the Biblical sense, an ointment is an oil-based balm that has medicinal properties and often has fragrances in it. For example, the Balm of Gilead in considered an ointment. You would anoint a person with an ointment to bring healing. In the medical world today, an ointment like Neosporin, would contain an antibiotic to kill germs and often has an anesthetic in it to relieve pain. When we listen to anointed preaching and teaching, it can be a spiritual ointment for our soul. The anointing can remove germs and reduce pain. Being in an anointed atmosphere can bring healing for the soul.

5) When we have done these things, then, we are ready for the bandage. A physical wound needs to be checked, treated, and dressed daily until it is healed. We should do the same with our emotional wounds. We can't assume that once we have emotionally processed a painful event, that bitterness may not try to take root later. We need to check our heart daily to make sure infection of unforgiveness or bitterness doesn't start to fester.

A New Season

I believe we will be entering a new season where God is going to be healing hearts. He is going to be healing the big stuff and the little stuff. I believe we are about to witness a move of God that will encompass emotional healing, physical healing, deliverance, spiritual authority, faith, and salvation. Emotional healing will move from the background to the foreground. It will have as much emphasis as the other teachings that God will be highlighting in this next move of God.

I believe this emotional healing move of God is going to be similar to the healing revivals of the 50's. God used hundreds of ministers to flow in the gifts of healing. Some of them were healed themselves at an early age.

Oral Roberts was the most famous healing preacher during the healing revivals of the 50's. He was well-known because he was on television. Prior to his televised program, healing was mostly taught within Pentecostal churches. However, Oral Roberts was the one that delivered the message of healing to the general public through his TV programs.

Oral Roberts almost died from tuberculosis as a teenager. God healed him and he received his calling when he was healed. His testimony helped strengthen the faith in his audience and it helped him operate in faith.

Just like Oral Roberts was physically healed early in life and God used him to preach about it, I believe the same will be true with emotional healing. There are many that God has healed emotionally, and they are called to minister emotional healing in this next move of God.

God used more than a dozen well-known names during the healing revival of the 50's but there were hundreds of other pastors that God used to bring healing to people. I believe the same will be true with this new wave of emotional healing. There will be some well-known names but there will be hundreds of other pastors that will flow mightily in releasing emotional healing to their congregation.

How will people receive emotional healing? I believe it will flow the same ways that physical healings are released.

1) **Sovereignly.** God will just zap people healed.

2) **Laying on of hands.** God will use pastors and church elders to be conduits for healing.

3) **By Faith.** People have the ability to use their faith for healing and miracles. This includes emotional healing. A person needs to get a revelation of their healing and allow it to sink down into their heart (subconscious mind).

4) **A Special Anointing.** Ministers will have a *word of knowledge* for specific things. As well, God may give some ministers an unusual or distinctive anointing for certain soul conditions.

5) **Through Laughter.** We have seen this happen in Rodney Howard-Brown's meetings and we have seen it in some of Kenneth Hagin's meetings. There have been several services where spontaneous laughter has broken out. During those services, God made heart adjustments, deposited impartations, and healed emotional wounds (as well as physical ailments).

6) **Through Tears.** This happened to me. In 2003, I was at a women's leadership retreat, and I started crying

for no reason. When I asked God why I was crying, a memory came to mind of an incident in my life that happened eight years earlier. It was a challenging situation where I was yelled at, scorned, and rejected. I didn't know that I still carried an emotional wound from that day. But God told me that my tears were part of my soul healing from that event.

There was another time that Roberts Liardon was preaching in Africa to 5,000 people and spontaneous weeping broke out across the auditorium. I was watching the service via livestream. When Pastor Roberts said "Restore," weeping broke out, and the Holy Spirit told me that God was healing emotional wounds in the people there.

7) **Through Baptism.** A new anointing through baptism sprang up in February of 2018 and the North Georgia Revival was birthed. Numerous physical healings and emotional healings have taken place as people were water baptized at Christ Fellowship Church in Dawsonville, Georgia. Healings through water baptism have spread to other churches and territories.

These are the seven ways I believe God will be healing hearts in the next move of God. There may be additional avenues of healing, but these are the ones that I have knowledge of at this time.

God Zapped Me

When I first started to write this book, I sensed that the Holy Spirit wanted me to share my experience with emotional healing. I was fine with that. I want people to know what God did for me because He will certainly do it for others.

God zapped my heart healed on August 8, 1994. I had just rededicated by life back to God in June of 1994, after being backslidden for nearly ten years. I was attending the Vineyard Church of Newport Beach. Prior to August 8th, I would sit in the church services by myself and just cry. I was heartbroken from a break-up with a boyfriend in June. I was still devastated over Fred's suicide almost a year and a half earlier. My best friend Sharon had moved out of state a couple of months earlier. And I was no longer working at a company that I had given my blood, sweat, and tears to for the previous six years. All my friends worked at that company, and I was no longer in communication with them. I was alone, lonely, and broken.

I went to church Sunday morning on August 8th and I came home and took a nap. When I woke up from the nap, I heard in my spirit, "Go get baptized."

What? Why was God telling me to get baptized? I was baptized when I was seven or eight years old. I opened the bulletin from that morning. It said that there was going to be a baptism at someone's house that afternoon. I heard in my spirit, "Go." So, I jumped out of my bed, threw on pool appropriate clothes and a change of clothes for after, and drove to the address in the bulletin.

I didn't know anyone at that church. When I got to the house, there were about 30 people there. About ten of them were there to get baptized and the others were spectators. I got baptized, and then went to the Sunday night service at the Vineyard that evening.

At the end of the Sunday night service, the pastor asked those that had been baptized that day to come forward for prayer. I went forward and a few people gathered around me to pray. At that church, they didn't touch you when they prayed for you; they just extended their hands towards you. The next thing I knew, I was on the ground. I had been *slain in the spirit*.

As I laid there, I was vaguely aware that music was playing in the background. My eyes were closed, and I saw different colors of laser lights shooting across my eye lids.

A couple of days later, I asked God about that experience. I asked why there were laser lights on the inside of my eyelids.

The Holy Spirit said, "I was doing laser surgery on your heart."

Then, it dawned on me; my emotional pain was gone. The things that used to hurt didn't hurt anymore. The break-up with Patrick didn't hurt. Fred's suicide didn't hurt. Sharon moving out of state didn't hurt. I didn't feel alone and lonely. I didn't cry through the church services anymore. I was happy and felt happy.

My Birthday Calling

Later in August, I suddenly found myself enrolled in a Bible School. I won't go into all the details of that right now. However, on my 30th Birthday, on December 12, 1994, before I went to bed, I thought I would read my Bible a little bit. The scripture address of Zechariah 3 came up in my spirit, so I turned there and started reading. As soon as I began reading, a glory cloud filled my room and verses 1 through 8 literally glowed off the page. There was light beaming out of my Bible and the presence of God was tangible in my room. I was awake all night and I wept all night. The passage talked about Joseph, the High Priest, having dirty garments and the Angel of the Lord gave him clean clothes and a new turban on his head. God used that passage to tell me I was called into ministry. Even though I was enrolled in a Bible school, I didn't necessarily plan on going into ministry. I was in the Bible school out of obedience. I didn't mind working for God in an administrative roll or something, but I wasn't planning on having a pulpit or writing ministry. I understood that the dirty garments in the passage symbolized the secret shame that I carried. I felt dirty and unworthy to be called into ministry because of the abortions I had had. I cried out to God telling Him that He didn't want me because I had *skeletons in my closet*. I didn't want to bring reproach to God.

In May of 1995, an instructor in the Bible School told us to ask God if there was anything stopping us from stepping into our destiny. I asked the question, and I heard in my spirit, "Pride." Right after that, I found myself ostracized from the Bible School and on a journey to study pride since I didn't understand how it could possibly be in my life.

In July of 1995, I attended the West Coast Believers convention and between the services, a woman approached me and told me that God had just told her to give me the phrase and concept, "Diseases of the Soul." She said God was going to teach it to me and I would teach it to the body of Christ.

I had several dramatic supernatural experiences in the 90's. (I will share a few more in this chapter). But first, I want to delve into why God directed me to include by birthday calling experience in this chapter on emotional healing.

To be honest, I was apprehensive about sharing that experience and others I will write about in this chapter. However, I know God directed me to talk about them. I believe the reason God wanted me to write about my birthday calling is He is wanting to highlight secret shame. My calling encounter wasn't just about me. I believe there are many people who think their past makes them unqualified or disqualified for ministry. And maybe that is true by the world's standards, but not Gods.

I was carrying secret shame. Are you carrying shame from an event in your past? The very thing you are most ashamed of can be the thing that God will use to show the world His grace and redemption. What is your secret shame? Whatever you did doesn't have to define who you are today. Is there something financial, sexual, or even illegal that you are ashamed of?

My secret shame was abortions. I know there will be plenty of people that will forever judge me and hold me in derision for the actions I took in my youth. There are others that will extend grace towards me since my actions were decades ago. However, when I had my dramatic calling experience, it had only been about two and a half years (summer of '92 to Dec. of '94) since Fred and I made the decision to end my pregnancy.

God, in a very dramatic way, labeled me as righteous. As the passage says, He removed my filthy garments and gave me a white robe to wear.

Back then, there was only one woman on Christian TV that admitted to having an abortion. And every time she spoke about it, she appeared to have to repent all over again trying to get the viewers to not hate her. She didn't demonstrate a woman that walked in righteousness. She acted like and was treated like a woman that would forever carry the shame of the actions she took in her youth.

I know there are people reading this that are carrying secrets they are ashamed of. They don't talk about them. They have the memory and the shame of their actions buried in a nook and cranny of their heart.

For some of you, God is telling you that you are not disqualified from ministry, happiness, or blessings. Stop self-sabotaging to punish yourself.

There are others that your secret shame is the reason for your depression, and it is the area that your demons focus their harassment on. They whisper suicidal thoughts and tell you what a terrible person you are.

When we surrender our life to God and accept Jesus in our hearts, our ugly past is erased in the eyes of God. He sees us as righteous and worthy of His love and favor.

If you don't see yourself in a white rob and you are still carrying around your filthy garments, I encourage you to study the topic of spiritual righteousness until you get a revelation of it down into your subconscious mind. Please, lift your head. You are forgiven. You are released from the shackles of your past.

Remember, if we can't talk about a past wound, then we aren't healed from it. God wants total healing in this season. The devil doesn't get to keep us bound to shame any longer.

The Angelic Visitation

This is another dramatic spiritual encounter I believe God wants me to share. I started attending my sister Stephanie's church, Cottonwood Christian Center, and she wanted me to go with her to a women's retreat in July of 1995.

I agreed to go to the retreat, even though I didn't know anyone except my sister. Stephanie had somehow signed me up to perform stand-up comedy at the Saturday night session at the outside amphitheater. I was a little nervous about it because I was trying out new material and the vein the conference had lots of weeping. I didn't understand why I would be doing comedy for women that had spent two days crying.

That Saturday afternoon, they had a "quiet time" planned where everyone was supposed to go off by themselves and spend time with God. I took my Bible and sat in the Amphitheater. I decided to re-read the chapter that I had read that morning which was Isaiah 42.

All the sudden, I looked up from my Bible, and a pure white hummingbird was hoovering a foot away from my face. Its face looked kind of human, and it was shining love and compassion towards me. The hummingbird had light beams coming from it. It looked like it could have been a special effect out of a movie. So, to reiterate, this creature had light beams coming from it, it had a face with human-like characteristics, and it was somehow conveying love and compassion towards me.

At that point, it dawned on me that the hummingbird was an angelic visitation. After I had that realization, I heard in my spirit, "Be encouraged." The angel then gave me a knowing acknowledgement, then flew away.

For the rest of the retreat, two pure white hummingbirds followed me everywhere I went when I was outside. When I went from the chapel to the cabin, they followed.

When I went from the cabin to the mess hall, they were there, either flying next to me or behind me as I walked.

I found out years later that there isn't a species of hummingbirds that is pure white. There is a white hummingbird with a red band around its neck in Georgia but nothing here in California. There are albino hummingbirds, but they would have had red eyes. These weren't albino. They had pigment in their eyes and on their legs.

Anyway, after the hummingbird flew away at the amphitheater, I didn't know what to do, so I continued reading my Bible where I left off. I read verses 6 and 7 of Isaiah 42, and I had a knowing in my spirit that God was highlighting those two verses.

The verses read, *"I, the Lord, have called you in righteousness, and will hold your hand; I will keep you and give you as a covenant to the people, as a light to the Gentiles, to open blind eyes, to bring out prisoners from the prison, those who sit in darkness from the prison house."*

We know this passage is prophetically talking about Jesus, but it also applies to us, the church, in this season. Isaiah 42:6-7 has a lot to unpack.

First, it says, *"I have called you in righteousness."* God already called me righteous during my birthday calling encounter. We have been made righteous and we have been given white robes which symbolize righteousness. The birthday calling event happened seven months before this hummingbird angel thing. Was God trying to emphasize it to me again?

After I got home from the retreat, I thought about it. I got the sense that there was a deeper level of understanding that God had in store for me. I then came to the realization that I still carried secret shame. I wasn't free in that area. God called me righteous, but I didn't feel righteous.

It was at that point that realized that I didn't remember a lot of details about my abortions. And I became aware that I had never emotionally processed that dark stain in my life. God had healed my heart supernaturally a year earlier, on August 8, 1994, with the laser surgery on my heart. Events in my life that used to hurt didn't hurt anymore and that was still true a year later. However, the abortion issue was different. The abortion issue was hidden matter. That wasn't an area of emotional pain because it was topic I had locked away in a dark corner of my heart. I never allowed myself to think about it. I had been in a form of denial about it.

So, in 1995, I went through a season (a couple of months) where I allowed God to help me emotionally process that hidden room of my heart. Yes, it was a season of repentance, and mourning for my children, but it was also a season of remembering. I made myself recount the details of my abortions and I journalized them. I wrote down the different types of fears that I dealt with at the time. I discovered that demons aggressively bombard young women with fear when they are pregnant. Demonic suggestions try to convince young people that they don't have a choice. The full-on mental assault of fears was relentless with the first pregnancy. So much so that when I found myself pregnant again a year later, I went into autopilot mode and repeated my actions. I didn't allow myself to think about it or express any emotion. I didn't consider that I had a choice in the matter. Afterall, all issues and options had been reviewed a year before when I was pregnant, and my situation hadn't changed. I, metaphorically, put my pregnancy experiences in a storage box, taped it up, and put it into a storage room in my soul. It didn't get opened. That is why I had to force myself to remember the details because I never allowed myself to before the emotional processing season that I did in 1995.

I will write about this more in a future book about abortion, but I believe God wanted me to talk about secret shame. We are entering a season of emotional healing but there are some issues that some people will need to emotionally process first before the healing will come. We need to be the one that unlocks that room that we store all our secrets in. God isn't going to bust down doors in our soul that we have banned Him from. If we go back to the metaphor of the bandaged skinned knee, we need to uncover our wound, so God can clean it and put spiritual Neosporin on it.

Okay, back to the Isaiah 42 scripture. Verse 6 says, *"I will hold your hand."* Holding hands is an act of intimacy. A person doesn't normally hold hands with acquaintances or even their friends.

We typically see three main reasons why people hold hands. 1) They hold hands as an expression of intimacy. A boyfriend or girlfriend will grab the others hand as a way to feel close or demonstrate affection. 2) We also take hold of a person's hand to lead and protect them. A parent will hold hands with their child, so the child will walk where the parent goes and the parent is able to protect them. 3) We also grab a person's hand to demonstrate kindness, friendship, or empathy. Caregivers will often hold the hand of their elderly patients as a way of connecting with them and demonstrating that their attention is focused on them.

If we look at all three of these reasons why people hold hands, it gives us insight into why God is telling us that He is holding our hand. 1) God loves us and wants to express affection towards us. 2) We are His children, and He wants to guide us and protect us. and 3) He desires a connection with us. He wants us to know that His focus is on us.

The Isaiah 42 passage goes onto to say, *"I will keep you and give you as a covenant to the people, as a light to the gentiles,"* God will keep us. He will keep us safe. He will keep our head above water. He will keep His angels round about us. He will keep us in perfect peace when our mind is set on Him. He will give us as a *covenant to the people.* The word "covenant" doesn't just mean agreement or promise, it means a binding oath. Gods promises to us are sure. God isn't like a flakey parent that promises his kid a trip to Disneyland but then changes his mind because he's tired. God isn't moody or fickle. God takes His promises seriously and He will keep them. God will use our lives as examples of the ways He keeps His promises. *"As a light to the gentiles"* simply means that even the non-Christians will see that God keeps His promises. As well, the light of Christ that shines through us, will be seen by the non-believers.

The Isaiah 42:6-7 passage says, *"To open blind eyes, to bring out prisoners from the prison, those who sit in darkness from the prison house,"* Freeing people from their mental and emotional bondages is one of the major reasons why Jesus came. In fact, if we read Luke 4:18-19, we see that Jesus announced in the synagogue that He came to heal the brokenhearted and free those in emotional prisons.

Luke 4:18-19 says,
"The Spirit of the Lord God is upon Me,
Because the Lord has anointed Me,
To preach the gospel to the poor,
He has sent Me to heal the brokenhearted.
To proclaim liberty to the captive,
And recovery of sight to the blind,
To set at liberty those who are oppressed.
To proclaim the acceptable year of the Lord."

After Jesus read the passage that was taken from Isaiah 61, He said, *"This day, this scripture is fulfilled in your ears."*

Yes, Jesus healed people physically and cast demons out of them. But one of His main assignments was to heal the brokenhearted. And we are instructed to follow Jesus' example and do what He did. Ministering to the oppressed and brokenhearted was a priority for Jesus and it should be for us as well.

And finally, what did the Holy Spirit say when I realized it was an angelic visitation? He said, "Be encouraged."

The definition of the word *encourage* is to give someone 1) support, 2) confidence, or 3) hope. I believe this is a word to us in this season.

Support. God is saying that He will support us. He will help us, provide for us, defend us, hold us, carry us, advocate for us, and strengthen us.

Confidence. God will give us confidence. He will give us an assurance, a certainty, a conviction, and a strength.

Hope. Isn't it interesting that *hope* is one of the words used in the definition of encourage? Depression is the caused from hopelessness. I believe God will be restoring hope in this season like never before. The discouraged will have recovery of sight to the blind. They will see good again. They will embrace hope again.

And finally, *be encouraged* can also mean to *take courage*. I believe we, the church, will rise up in boldness and confidence to call down demonic activity when we see it. Fears will greatly diminish as we step into a boldness anointing to carry out the assignments God has for us.

The Earring

Another unusual incident, that I believe God wants me to share, happened in the summer of 1996. My friend Betty and I were sitting in the parking garage at the Anaheim Convention Center after an evening service of a West Coast Believer's Convention. We were stuck in the parking garage because there were too many cars trying to leave at the same time.

Back then, it was the fashion to wear big earrings. By the end of a long day, those big earrings made your ears hurt. I took off my earrings and something very strange happened. The front of the earring had a post in it, but the back of the earring also had a post in it. I showed it to Betty, and we were both bewildered.

How did the earring get two posts? I double-checked both posts. It wasn't like the paint on the post separated and stayed with the back of the earring, giving the illusion that there were two posts. No. I checked them. They were both solid posts.

After I dropped Betty off at her apartment, I asked God about it. Why did my pierced earring have two posts?

God told me, "The things that have pierced you, I will heal in others."

God used that incident to tell me that my life is supposed to be an open book. I am supposed to share my experiences. I am not allowed to have areas of secret shame. I am supposed to discuss my heartaches, disappointments, and *skeletons in the closet* because He was going to use those experiences to help bring understanding to others.

Revelation 12:11 says, *"And they overcame him by the blood of the lamb and by the word of their testimony, and they did not love their life unto death."*

In this season, we shouldn't underestimate what God can do when we share both the good and bad details of our life. I believe the word that God will heal the things that have pierced me doesn't just apply to me. God knew He would have me write about that experience decades later. I believe God did that "sign and wonder' of making a second earring post appear, because He wants to heal hearts in this season. If there are areas of secret shame, God wants us to get a revelation that we are made righteous by the "blood of the lamb." As well, God will be prompting many to give their testimony. As the verse suggests, we will defeat the wiles of the devil by sharing our story. We overcome the evil one by the word of our testimony.

I know most people have details of their life that they would prefer not to share. I understand that. We don't want to be judged or scorned. However, I believe we are stepping into a season of emotional healing. That experience we are ashamed of can bring freedom and liberation to someone else. I encourage to you to ask God if it is time to share some of the stuff that has been buried in that closet of your heart.

What's in a Name?

The last experience I believe God wanted me to write about happened in 1997. I was reading my Bible and the Holy Spirit asked me, "What is your name?"

I said, "Deborah."

He said, "Who was Deborah?"

I said, "A mother of Israel."

He said, "What does Deborah mean?"

I said, "Bee."

He said, "What do bees produce?"

I said, "Honey."

He said, "What do mothers produce?"

I said, "Milk."

Then He said, "I am going to use you to help take My people into the land of milk and honey. That which you produce will help take My people into their promised land."

I hadn't been studying milk, honey, or the meaning of Deborah at that time. Those things weren't on my radar. However, I understood that day, that what the Holy Spirit had just told me wasn't just about monetary blessing (although it included money). It was about shalom. Shalom means wholeness, completeness, soundness, health, safety, prosperity, and peace. I understood that day that God wanted to use me to help His people find their peace and emotional healing.

I believe there are two reasons that God wanted me to share this experience.

1) I believe God emphasized my name because He is calling many into their namesake. I believe I am one of the Deborahs He will be using in the coming season. But He will be raising up several Deborahs even if their given name isn't Deborah. He will be raising up Esthers that were born for such a time as this. Their radical obedience will change their nation. He will raise up Marys who will carry, birth, and nurture strategies and programs that will bring salvation and deliverance to people. I believe we will see prophets rise up that will carry a spirit of Elijah. We will also see delivers come on the scene that will carry a spirit of Moses, that will lead their people group out of bondage and into the promises of God. I also believe there will be several that will embody of characteristics of Joseph. Their divine strategies will bring provision in times of drought and famine.

In addition to Biblical anointings and mantles, I believe we will see mantles of some of the generals of faith that have passed on, rest on ministers in this new move of God. Their mantles, anointings, and giftings will flow through well-known and unknown five-fold ministers in this new season.

2) The second reason I believe God wanted me to share this experience is, He wants you to know that your "promise land" is still possible. So many people have lost hope. They have been through so much loss. They don't dare even think about the promises that they felt God

had whispered to them at one point in their life. Consider for a moment that your promise land is possible and obtainable. I believe it's time to hope again. The word God gave me is saying that millions of believers will be stepping into their promise land. Praise God!

It's About God

I acknowledge the experiences mentioned in this chapter are pretty dramatic, but these encounters aren't about me. I am one of many that God will be using in this season. God wants to clean house. He wants to heal hearts. He wants to purge secret shame. He wants His people healthy, healed, and whole both physically and emotionally.

If you are reading this and the Holy Spirit is bearing witness with you that He wants to use you as a minister for emotional healing, understand that God had to take you through a season of humility. The people that God uses in this new season, whether that be for physical healing, emotional healing, or anything else, will have had to go through a season of dying to self. They will have had their pride squeezed out by circumstances and events that were difficult at the time.

God plans to do miracles through His people in this season and the people God uses in significant ways can't have excessive pride in their heart. 1) Pride leads to deceptive thinking. 2) Pride hampers discernment to hear from God clearly. 3) And pride wants to take the glory that belongs to God alone.

God's servants must walk in humility of heart yet carry a boldness and authority in the spirit realm. If you are reading this, I suspect that God has been nudging you towards your calling. Don't dismiss thoughts that seem too big or too grand. God may very well be giving you a vision of what He wants for your life. Simply trust and obey and see where God takes you.

If You Struggle with Depression

If you are a person that has struggled with depression your whole life, seek God. Get in church every time the doors are open. Let God know you want emotional healing. And after you receive it, don't be surprised if God calls you to be a vessel of His healing power. If you can, keep a diary and journalize your thoughts and struggles. God wants to give you insights that He will want you to share with others later to help them in their struggles.

Truly, a brighter day is on the horizon. Lift your gaze and seek God. You will be amazed at the wonderful surprises God has in store for you.

www.ingramcontent.com/pod-product-compliance
Lightning Source LLC
Chambersburg PA
CBHW060534130626
46553CB00002B/752